DISAPPEARING APPALACHIA IN TENNESSEE

DISAPPEARING APPALACHIA IN TENNESSEE

A PICTURE OF A VANISHED LAND AND ITS PEOPLE

HARRY MOORE & FRED BROWN

Published by The History Press
Charleston, SC
www.historypress.com

Unless otherwise noted, all photographs are by Harry Moore.

First published 2021

Manufactured in the United States

ISBN 9781467149433

Library of Congress Control Number: 2021931156

To Jeanne McDonald, life partner, a fabulous award-winning author, editor and precious soul who is vastly missed.
—Fred Brown

To my late mother and father, Agnes and Leander Moore.
To Charles Cavin, a Tennessean from Appalachia who greatly aided our efforts in researching this book.
—Harry Moore

CONTENTS

PREFACE

Gray dust swirls and floats into the breeze after a car passes on the country gravel road. Fine grayish-white particles, pale as clay, settle over the honeysuckle and tree leaves reminiscent of a light snow dusting. As I walk along that gravel road, I kick at gravel in the roadbed, trying to see how far I can move them with my foot. A crow begins to announce in a crow's particular way that I am nearby, and a rabbit bounds from the roadside honeysuckle, crosses the road and hops into the adjacent dust-covered pasture. I remember those days long ago when as a child I sauntered down this road in front of my grandparents' house out in the country. Those days are pretty much gone, disappearing as fast as the dust along a country road.

The disappearance of portions of our American culture is a never-ending occurrence. Some things vanish quickly as technology increases. Other parts of our culture change slowly, evolving as people encounter new and changing attitudes, concerns, difficulties and the resistance-to-change traditions. Still other portions of our culture are blended as people migrate from one section of our great country to another, combining their previous cultural characteristics with the new.

Distinct characteristics of a culture can identify certain groups of people, where they live, what their heritage consists of, what they might eat and where they might attain spiritual identity, to name a few. We often hear of the old southern drawl or the New England accent or the Brooklyn fast talk. Each region of our nation has distinguishing characteristics that make those areas and their people unique, special and enduring.

Above: The Appalachian landscape varies from mountainous to ridges and valleys to high tabletop plateau lands. Pictured here is a view of Clinch Mountain from Copper Ridge in Powder Springs, Tennessee.

Opposite, top: Most housing in Appalachia is of wood construction. Early nineteenth-century houses were mostly log-type houses. In the early twentieth century, they were more likely to be wood-frame construction, as pictured here.

Opposite, bottom: This is the metal seat section for a tobacco setter that was discarded and abandoned to the weeds and brush along Bullen Valley Road in northern Grainger County. Mechanical tobacco setters were once in widespread use in the Appalachian region when burley tobacco was a common crop on the family farm.

To capture those special elements about a region of our country is a daunting task, not to be taken lightly. As such, our efforts with this book are to document certain aspects about the Appalachian culture that have disappeared or are fast becoming a thing of the past as change rolls into our everyday life. It is the special way we talk, the good home "country cooking" we devour, the solitary family life of the country farmer we cherish and the patriotic and faithful attitudes we hold dear that make Appalachia so unique—in other words, our people and our culture.

In order to accomplish this mission, the authors canvassed the Appalachian landscape to find people willing to discuss and talk about their heritage and upbringing: things that they used to do but now are fading from the scene. Some parts of the culture have disappeared completely while other practices are barely hanging on.

Most of the people interviewed for this project were of a mature age and remembered how Appalachian life used to be, how they were raised in log cabins, lived off the land; most had no electricity until the late 1930s. They remember seeing their first telephone, radio and television. All were proud patriotic Americans and wanted to have a good, honest life with happiness and freedom.

The authors have attempted to describe the landscape and how it came to be, how the people settled here and whence they came, what agriculture and farm life were like in the early twentieth century and what influences changed their way of life.

Many farmsteads are now abandoned and falling into disrepair across the Appalachian region, marking the slow disappearing phase of a culture known for hard work and love of the land.

In addition, we have attempted to capture certain aspects of the Appalachian culture with the aid of black-and-white photography. Photographs of certain aspects of the Appalachian life are told in shades of black and white with gray blending the two. Although the photographs may not fully cover the breadth of the subjects, we feel that a photograph saves a thousand words of print and acknowledges the importance of those topics of Appalachia.

Writing about the Appalachian life and culture includes many issues and activities, groups of people and events that would enlarge this narrative to encyclopedia size. We chose instead to focus on the Appalachian way of life experienced in East Tennessee during the first half of the twentieth century.

Certain topics of East Tennessee history have been thoroughly studied and described by many previous authors and researchers, topics such as Native American peoples, the Tennessee Valley Authority, coal mining and tobacco, just to name a few. In the narrative that follows we have briefly described those issues and subjects that lie outside of the scope of our discussion.

Much has been written by authoritative scholars about the early peoples of the land of Appalachia. Volumes of research data and published studies have clearly documented much of the Native American existence, culture

Above: Relics of a time when trucks were used for delivery and farm work, these old hulks can be found dotting the rural landscape in the valleys and along the ridges of East Tennessee. Most of these old cars have disappeared, being crushed and recycled into "new" metal for new cars.

Right: Trucks were once a mainstay of rural areas in Appalachia. They were mainly used for farm work and rural-type business like logging and mining. This old early 1940s Chevy truck was found edging out of an old rotting barn.

One of the many cultural icons of our past is the old stone chimney that remains long after the original structure is decayed and gone.

Old log barns were commonplace in East Tennessee during the 1800s until about the mid-1900s. These old structures are fast fading and represent a time in our cultural past when agriculture was a dominant part of every household.

and way of life in the Appalachian lands. Their special and honorable way of life was balanced with the natural world in that they were a part of the world around them.

A large area of Appalachia is underlain by vast deposits of coal, and the Appalachian economy was an integral part of the coal industry. The significance of coal and the people who mined the coal is not overlooked by the authors. In fact, we acknowledge their contribution to the way of life in not only Appalachia but also throughout the United States, as Appalachian coal was and is still being used by many sectors of America.

Another product of great importance to Appalachia was tobacco. At one time, most rural people grew tobacco not only to sell but also for personal use. It was a common practice for Appalachian folk to smoke or chew tobacco and even for some to dip snuff. Many families paid their taxes, bought clothes or a new car or tractor and sent the younger ones to school and college on the proceeds from selling their tobacco. It was a legal cash crop.

However, there were dangers associated with the use of tobacco products, which eventually took the lives of many across our country. The awareness of these dangers and the suffering that came with those dangers gradually pushed tobacco out of favor with the public, along with the loss of federal government subsidies for growing tobacco.

The area of Appalachia located in Tennessee and adjoining states became the focus of a new federal program that eventually became an energy production agency using hydroelectric and coal to nuclear energy. The Tennessee Valley Authority was formed in the early 1930s to help reduce and control flooding and erosion along the Tennessee River Valley and its tributaries in the Appalachian region. A number of concrete dams and resulting lakes were constructed along the Tennessee River and its tributaries, which in turn flooded many thousands of fertile acreages in the Appalachian region that had been commonly used to produce food crops.

The success of the TVA program was immeasurable and changed the Tennessee part of Appalachia forever. The flooding was brought under control, erosion was greatly reduced, electricity produced by the dam's hydroelectric capacity introduced electric power to most areas of Appalachia in Tennessee and adjacent regions for the first time and, finally, a recreation component began to grow with fishing, boating, swimming and relaxation on the newly constructed lakes. The TVA was and continues today to be a great asset of Appalachia.

Special aspects of Appalachia that have touched most families include such things as the Civilian Conservation Corps (CCC) and their work in the Great Smoky Mountains and large sections of the Cherokee National Forest, furniture making, music and the spirituality of churches and their congregations. Most of the folks from this region know about the craftsmanship that resides here: the potters, wood carvers, weavers and seamstresses, furniture makers, those who fashion musical instruments out of wood and congregations of faithful souls, to name a few of those special folks.

In addition, other types of industry, including the mining of zinc, fluorite, ball clay, marble and limestone creating products such as road gravel, concrete mix and aggregate, all have played a large role in the development of Appalachia and the culture along the way. Of course, there were those makers of moonshine who produced corn whiskey out in the mountain hollows and deep woods that provided the necessary medicinal tonics for those afflicted.

There is no doubt that the Appalachian region was an economically depressed area in the nineteenth and early twentieth centuries, all but forgotten after the Civil War and left to fend for itself as Reconstruction began to revitalize the country. The disappearance of some aspects of

Appalachia has been a good thing for the people of the region. Muddy roads, eroded lands, subsistence living, substandard housing and a virtually nonexistent healthcare network that existed in the 1800s and early 1900s are all things that have disappeared, and all are glad of it.

The introduction of electricity, employment, paved roads, healthcare and the availability of products have all been good for the people of Appalachia. Certain things about the past, including their work ethic, character, common sense approach to life, industriousness, faith, music, craftsmanship and family unity, to name a few, are all good things that have come out of Appalachia. But as time continues its march forward, there are certain aspects of Appalachia that are disappearing as a result.

We, the authors, felt the need to try to capture the way of life in Appalachia that is changing, disappearing, by using words and photographs. The interviews we obtained in our study and documentation efforts for this book project are priceless. Some of those we interviewed have passed away and soon more will be gone as well. With these deaths, a way of life and their memories go with them; encyclopedias of their way of life, their memories, lore and images are vanishing forever.

ACKNOWLEDGEMENTS

This book would not have been possible without many wonderful people of East Tennessee who opened their homes, farms and family histories to Fred Brown and Harry Moore.

The journey through East Tennessee backroads was not only a breathtaking adventure but also produced a greater insight into the history of this magnificently colorful region of the state and nation.

In addition, Fred Brown personally acknowledges his late wife, Jeanne McDonald, who died in 2019. Jeanne added her astute writing and editing skills in the early editing on this book. She was a retired editor at the University of Tennessee's former Center for Business and Economic Research, an award-winning novelist and short story author.

Also, Fred's daughter, Sumner Gibbs, worked on an earlier version of the book as well, giving sage advice to the final product. She is a technical writer and editor for Oak Ridge National Laboratory.

And lastly, Fred acknowledges Steve Cotham, manager of the Calvin M. McClung Historical Collection, the genealogy and history research branch of the Knox County Public Library System, and Cherel B. Henderson, executive director of the East Tennessee Historical Society, as such reliable resources for him over many years. Plus, Fred thanks the *Knoxville News-Sentinel*, where he spent over two decades as a reporter. The regional newspaper allowed him the privilege of roaming East Tennessee in search of history and regional stories for many years.

Without this help, the writing of this book would be incomplete.

In addition, Harry and Fred are especially grateful to the late Inez Adams for sharing her wonderful old photographs of her life growing up in Cades Cove. Thanks also goes to Lois Caughron and her family for providing photographs of their life and times in Cades Cove. In addition, special thanks go to Mary Gene Roberts for letting us use photos from her past to enrich this story. We also thank Linda Gass for use of her old photographs of Mill Springs Mill, later referred to as Cox Mill.

Our gratitude goes to the State of Tennessee State Library and Archives for the use of its historical photographs of the East Tennessee region, several of which we use and acknowledge in the book.

A special personal acknowledgement from us goes to Charles Cavin, who was instrumental in guiding us to several places and people in East Tennessee that are discussed in this story. His knowledge of the people and their effect on the Appalachian way of life greatly aided our efforts.

One of the people who had to struggle with our manuscript and smooth the edges was Amy Spencer, a freelance writer and editor. We are grateful to her and her efforts to improve our writing.

We are also indebted to Steve Sutton for his help with formatting our manuscript and general review of the details of organizing our work.

We are indebted to The History Press and in particular Chad Rhoad and Abigail Fleming for their willingness to take this project to fruition. We thank you for publishing our work.

An incredibly special thank-you to Harry's wife, Alice Ann, for her encouragement and support through this endeavor. Her career with the University of Tennessee Institute of Agriculture as an Extension Agent, District Supervisor and State Director of the 4-H Youth Development Department provided an invaluable link for us to connect with people and information across the state of Tennessee.

INTRODUCTION

Growing up in Appalachia before, during and just after World War II was to live in a village in an age of innocence. Feed and seed stores were gathering places where old men cracked jokes and floors creaked and groaned under foot traffic. Small towns squatted around country landscapes where many roads were still dirt and gravel.

Hillsides rambled in great greenswards, rolling young and vibrant. Crops grew in a patchwork of greens and browns, yellows and whites. Tree lines identified huge swaths of a farmer's boundary. Or maybe a stacked rock wall isolated one section from another.

Common wood-shingled crib barns, tobacco barns or the exquisitely designed cantilevered barn were stalwart structures of the time. They stored hay, cattle and brown-leaf tobacco, hanging like drying leather from the rafters.

That was Appalachia of the pre- and postwar years. Not today.

"Disappearing farms is the biggest change I have seen in my lifetime," said the late Glenn Cardwell, eighty-three, who was born in historic Greenbrier, a green valley in the Great Smoky Mountains National Park, where he spent thirty-four years as a park ranger.

The valley of his youth was marked by small farms, smokehouses, gristmills, cornfields and pastureland, in reality a village life. But when the village disappears, so does the culture.

"I didn't know we were in a Depression," Cardwell said, remembering his childhood. "We made do or we did without. We were a sufficient society,

A variety of tobacco known as burley tobacco was once king in the Appalachian region. The tobacco stalk was "skewered" on a thin stick, which was then impaled into the ground for a few days of initial drying before being placed in the tobacco barn.

even though it was hand-to-mouth. It was a good life," added Cardwell, who formerly served as the mayor of picturesque Pittman Center near Sevierville, Tennessee, a mountain village that holds its mountain heritage close.

"Losing the farms has changed our way of life," Cardwell acknowledged. "The other thing that changed us is that the government bought up the farmer's allotments of tobacco. Now, our tobacco barns are empty."

Today, tourism is king in East Tennessee, especially near Sevierville, Pigeon Forge and Gatlinburg, the small mountain town nestled in the bosom of the National Park. "There was no commerce in those early days. It was rural, wherever you looked."

Not today. Commerce, as Cardwell noted, has pushed aside whole farms and farmlands. Instead of growing crops, acres of land in East Tennessee today grow houses. In the case of Pigeon Forge and Gatlinburg, motels, tourist-oriented recreation and entertainment have sprouted like mushrooms.

But East Tennessee is not the only part of Appalachia that is facing rapid change. So is the land itself of the Grand Division of West Tennessee for comparison.

Serene pastures roll and tumble after spring hay cutting in Appalachia. Rectangular hay bales have mostly been replaced with the larger round bales seen here.

A farmer cultivates his tobacco crop using a small tractor. Tobacco crops are mostly gone from the Appalachian landscape.

The late Paul Richardson was ninety-two years old at the time of this interview and a retired farmer and veteran of World War II who grew up and farmed in West Tennessee in Crockett County. He worked behind a pair of plow mules all day breaking up a field. Main crops, he said, were corn, cotton, hay and oats. He hand-chopped weeds out of the rows of cotton and picked the cotton by hand.

The biggest change in his life, he said, was the mechanization of farming. His family had four mules and farmed 50 acres in the 1920s and 1930s. Today, one man can farm 1,500 acres alone, using computers on exceptionally large equipment and understanding the intricacies of soil science, fertilizers and the mechanization of production.

Rural living during the 1930s and '40s was not easy. Homes did not have conveniences we take for granted: water was hauled from a well or cistern; heat derived from wood, oil or coal stove; light was from oil lamps; bathrooms were outhouses; and houses were rarely insulated.

In fact, Richardson said electricity arrived in his section of Crockett County in the late 1930s. In East Tennessee, the Tennessee Valley Authority, created in 1933, provided electricity for the region, bringing lights for the first time to many a darkened household.

Most all communities had a school, a church and a store, which sold all manner of necessities. But with the demise of the rural community school, Richardson noted, began the decay of the rural community. Education was highly valued, and schools were usually located in the center of the community, where children would not have to walk or ride a bicycle more than a few miles to attend. There were no carpools.

Community stores were commonplace in most rural areas, providing necessary staples like flour, sugar, meal, bacon and coffee. Many stores were a combination country store and hardware outlet. Some even bartered for fresh chickens and eggs and even sold caskets, nails, garden tools and barbed wire. And most stores offered credit throughout the year, relying on being paid after fall harvest season. Big-box chains run by giant brands have replaced the hardware and general-purpose store.

A very real perspective of the change in Appalachia concerns the number of farms and acreage in 1920 compared to the latest figures for today. In 1920, East Tennessee had roughly 76,376 farms on 6,129,296 acres compared to 32,139 farms on 3,443,405 acres today.

In general, said Dr. Tim Cross, dean of the University of Tennessee Extension in the UT Institute of Agriculture, farms are losing the battle to subdivisions, shopping centers and urban expansion. "The best farmland is

Left: Once a premier cash crop for the farmers of Appalachia, tobacco has all but disappeared due to the removal of federal subsidies. Pictured here is a pile of tobacco baskets that were used to stack bundles of the leaf crop to take to market.

Below: The old Grainger County Jail in Rutledge, Tennessee, constructed in 1845 and pictured here in 1980, was placed on the National Register of Historic Places in 2015.

An old-time manner of discarding one's automobile license plate was to nail it on the side of an outbuilding, garage or barn.

In Appalachia country and more specifically in East Tennessee, advertising on barn roofs and barn sidewalls was commonplace, as seen in this Rock City advertisement along U.S. Highway 11-W in Grainger County. *From* A Geologic Trip Across Tennessee by Interstate 40, *Moore, 1994, University of Tennessee Press.*

Left: Hams hang in a smokehouse as they are cured on a farm in Appalachia. Some hams were hickory smoke cured while others were salt cured; most were simply referred to as "country hams."

Below: The hull of a truck quietly rusts away on the edge of a corn field in rural East Tennessee.

Right: Tobacco baskets and old pulleys hang in a disused barn in rural East Tennessee.

Below: Craftsmanship abounds in Appalachia. This door brace on an outbuilding is an example of the artistic ability shown by the Appalachian people.

Gristmills were common in Appalachia during the nineteenth and early twentieth centuries, as most rural communities needed a place to grind their grain for food and livestock feed. Pictured here is the water wheel for French's Mill in Jefferson County, Tennessee.

the bottomland, and the best place to build a house is on flatlands. Clearly, all of agriculture has changed over the last fifty years and it's been revolutionary in many ways."

Technology, he said, allows fewer farmers to produce more food.

"That is good," added Cross. "It allows us to feed ourselves at lower costs. But the downside is that adoption of technology has largely favored the growth of larger farms. We have seen the consolidation of farms, and simultaneously the loss of farmland due to urbanization and housing development."

The old home place is passing into history in Appalachia as cities and towns spread their reach.

Like fog rolling in from a river, covering the low-lying land and blurring the nature of the countryside, change is altering the face of Appalachia. In reality, Appalachia is becoming just like its towns and cities, urban and cloaked in sameness.

PART I

BEGINNINGS

1

A BEAUTIFUL AND ANCIENT LAND

A thin distant smudge from the top of Mount Le Conte, a majestic mountain in the Great Smoky Mountains National Park (GSMNP), fades northerly in a long decline through a blue haze like a single pencil line being erased. It is a trail in time skipping across the saw tooth ridges of Webb Mountain, Shields Mountain, Bear Wallow Mountain and on into the beyond. Like an ancient traveler the sloping remnant has been there in beautiful isolation, defining our history in a language of stones from the dawn of time.

Geologists believe that line hovering in the sky to be the only reminder of an ancestral floor that supported this region two to twenty million years ago. Today, we live below the ancient floor, riding an erosional elevator to the bottom.

I have set out to recharge my soul from a high mountain top; earnestly and with purpose I seek the landscape views. The stillness and silence are deafening, the closeness to our spirit is magnetic. Forward I ascend to gain purpose and understanding.

As I climb the side of Clinch Mountain, I begin to recognize the hard sandstone outcropping along the animal path I am following. I know that the view from the top is stunning. The short huckleberry bushes brush against my calves as I near the top of the ridge. Large deep-furrowed bark dresses the trunk of old red oak trees that stand resolute on the south side of the ridge I am climbing. I can now see the valley below between openings in the tree limbs and bushes. Farmhouses, barns, fence rows and a two-lane winding road texture the landscape below as I climb higher and higher.

Clinch Mountain is a pronounced ridge that stretches from near the northeast Knox County line, through Grainger and Hawkins Counties on into southwest Virginia. It stands over one thousand feet above the adjacent valley floors on either side of the mountain. The crest is narrow with a very steep "north" side and a less steep sloping "south" side. The section of Clinch Mountain I am climbing is in Blaine, Tennessee, at the terminus of the mountain.

A strong warm breeze blows in my face, updrafts from the valley. I see several black vultures riding thermals above as the warm air rises. They circle in broad arcs, sometimes seeming to glide off the thermal to lower elevations to inspect something that caught their eye.

Farmhouses come into view as I look out from the trail to the low areas below the mountain; fence lines, pastures and small ponds dot the landscape. This rugged land has changed somewhat since it was first settled. A washboard of parallel ridges and intervening valleys begins to stretch out toward the east and west. Along the horizon I can see the outline of the Smoky Mountains to the east.

The peak of the mountain I now stand on is known locally as Signal Point. Hard sandstone outcrops, millions of years old, are prominent on this mountain peak; they are the reason that the mountain peak exists. The wind has picked up a bit and is coming out of the southwest; a front may be moving this way. I can clearly see the landscape all around me as I stand on this prominence and take in the views to the south, southwest and west, in a broad 180-degree arc.

The great mountains of the Blue Ridge where the Great Smoky Mountains National Park is located, as well as Cherokee National Forest and other mountain regions, seem like a bluish haze of outlined topography rising skyward in the east. From this peak I am standing on, I look across the great valley and see the "rippled" landscape of the valley and ridge where rivers join to form the mighty Tennessee River system. To the west and northwest lies the escarpment of the Cumberland Plateau, a prominent thousand-foot rise in the landscape that I can see from Clinch Mountain.

These are beautiful and distinctive landforms that characterize the topography of Appalachia. How did this come to be, and how did the Appalachian territory influence the culture of those who settled this wild and rugged land? How much has this land changed since it was first formed geologic eons ago?

Geologists tell a story of vast landmasses that moved around the planet forming supercontinents and then breaking apart into smaller pieces we

Right: Most of the rocks in the Blue Ridge Province of Appalachia started out as sedimentary in origin and have since been metamorphosed by heating and pressure from the collision of major continents some 230 million years ago. Shown is folded phyllite and metasiltstone along SR 416 in Sevier County, Tennessee.

Below: The more resistant rocks found in Appalachia tend to form bluffs and ledges, some of which are attractive and are destination points for hikers and outdoor enthusiasts, as shown here at Alum Cave Bluff in the Great Smoky Mountains National Park.

Sedimentary rocks, including these sandstone layers, known as the Devils Racetrack and seen from Interstate 75 in Campbell County, were turned vertically, folded and faulted many millions of years ago.

now recognize as continents today. Time is the constant in all of this that we see, not thousands of years but hundreds of millions of years and even several billion years. No doubt this land, and even this planet, has changed through time.

Since the formation of the rocks, the earth has relentlessly beaten down on them with rain, sleet, snow, ice, dust storms, fire storms and even earthquakes. All these agents have slowly changed the planet into what we see today.

A beautiful and ancient land, East Tennessee and the Appalachian Region hold a vast and rich heritage that is fast becoming but a mist of the past. A complex and long history of continent collisions and upheavals has transformed the region into a varied landscape of many forms, rock types and mineral deposits. These are the riches that the early settlers in the land we call Appalachia searched for and transformed into homesteads, plowshares and communities.

The topography of the Appalachian Region is rugged and varied. One can travel from the high mountains of the Blue Ridge to the many parallel ridges and valleys of that washboard topography in East Tennessee and

The rugged Appalachian Mountains are underlain by rocks, some of which are 1 billion years old. Other rocks are younger, with most being 250 to 500 million years old.

The rocks of Appalachia have weathered to form a varied topography and landscape, replete with beautiful mountains, ridges and valleys and waterfalls, such as the majestic 256-foot-high Fall Creek Falls along the escarpment of the Cumberland Plateau in Van Buren County, Tennessee.

One of the characteristics of the human impact on Appalachia is the tapping of hydroelectric power, which dramatically changed the lives of those living in Appalachia. Pictured here is Calderwood Dam, along the Tennessee and North Carolina border.

Virginia to the plateaus and chiseled coal mining terrain of Tennessee, Kentucky, West Virginia and Virginia.

Our story begins more than one billion years ago when a super landmass referred to as Rodinia was created by colliding landmasses called continents. That series of collisions resulted in a mountain-building episode known as the Grenville Orogeny and formed a super continent that scientists refer to as Rodinia. That landmass stood together for many millions of years, resisting the breakdown by weathering processes such as rain, wind, earthquakes, mass-wasting and ice, to name a few.

Approximately 700 to 800 million years ago, the continent of Rodinia, geologists say, broke apart as convection forces within the earth's mantle changed and formed new pathways for the surface crust to move across the globe. These very large sections of Rodinia eventually became continents of their own as they traveled around the earth's surface, being "drug" (propelled) by the flow of mantle convection (where the molten mantle material rises upward away from the core toward the crust and then as it cools moves back toward the earth's core in a repetitive cycle).

Upwelling of the hot mantle material formed new volcanoes in the oceans as the seafloors pulled apart. These volcanic regions connected and formed island arcs and later new mountains of igneous rocks, formed by the cooling of the hot lava or magma. The slow but steady movement of continental drift eventually led to the formation of another supercontinent.

As the great continents were traveling toward a major collision some 230 million years ago, rivers and streams deposited their eroded wealth into shallow seas and bays of the ever-closing waters between the continents. Lagoons, sandy beaches, barrier islands, bryozoan reefs, river deltas, land swamps (which would eventually form our coal deposits) and carbonate banks (not unlike those of the current-day Bahamas) were some of the environments in which these sediments originated and eventually formed the sedimentary rocks of the region.

In some places, pebbles and cobbles of harder minerals such as quartz were added to the mixture of sediments that lay on the ocean bottom. In time, these sediments were compressed and lithified into rock layers and masses. Most of these rocks were then deformed and metamorphosed into harder strata like meta-conglomerate, meta-siltstone, quartzite, slate, phyllite, gneiss and schist.

The past continents of Laurentia (the proto–North America) and Gondwanaland (what would eventually become Africa and South America) were later joined to form another supercontinent referred to by scientists as Pangea. This occurred some 230 million years ago and culminated in the Alleghanian Orogeny and the formation of the Appalachian Mountain range.

As the drifting continents continued their journey to form the supercontinent Pangea, the sediments that were deposited in the intervening environments and seas and streams were pushed together in an accordion-like style, resulting in their extreme deformation. Some of the strata were faulted, broken and forced over other sediments and rocks while others were simply folded into arch- and basin-like structures called anticlines and synclines. Some rocks were folded and faulted multiple times.

Pangea remained as a whole landmass for some thirty to fifty million years before being pulled apart by the ever-changing convection currents within the earth's mantle. As Pangea separated into distinct landmasses, the continents of North America, South America and Africa began to take shape in the form that we recognize today.

Approximately 200 million years of erosion, weathering, uplift of the land and subsequent downward erosion has taken place in Appalachia and continues to this very day. It is believed by geologist researchers today that

Most of the rocks in the Appalachian region are sedimentary in origin, beginning their existence as ocean sediments and consisting of sandstone, siltstone, shale and limestone.

This photo shows an excellent example of a thrust fault where the rock layers on the right have been shoved (thrusted) up and over the rocks on the left. This type of faulting is common in the Appalachians.

the current mountain topography has developed within the past seven to ten million years, marking a continued uplift of the landmass and subsequent erosion of the surface and rocks.

Several episodes of deep freeze and total thaw have occurred during those many millions of years. These are referred to by scientists as "glacial" and "intraglacial" periods. The last glacial episode to leave its mark on North America, the Pleistocene epoch, ended some ten thousand years ago, and the earth has been warming ever since then. We are currently living in an intraglacial period.

What we now know as the Appalachian Mountains is the remaining mountain chain and rugged landscape that resulted from the Alleghanian Orogeny. The areas of land that we call Appalachia today include the Blue Ridge, Valley and Ridge and Appalachian Plateaus provinces. These provinces are found in parts of ten states: Georgia, Alabama, South Carolina, Tennessee, North Carolina, Kentucky, Virginia, West Virginia, Maryland and Pennsylvania.

As humans (*Homo sapiens*) developed and spread across the many continents of the earth, they adapted to the changing climates and landscape. First were the hunters and then the gatherers, as they would follow wild game

Some of the earliest known organisms were marine algae, and their presence was preserved in rocks as thin concentric layers known as stromatolites, shown here from Union County, Tennessee.

Fossils of animals can be found in many of the rock layers of Appalachia, such as the trilobite shown here, a cousin of the well-known horseshoe crab common today.

across the landscape and collect the wild fruits, nuts and berries for their sustenance. Later, agriculture developed as people learned to grow the plants they needed for food.

The Agricultural Revolution transformed the planet as societies developed around agricultural centers and produced food for their families. Native peoples understood their connection with the land and the animals and plants that lived there, and they created agrarian life.

The people who lived on Appalachian land had a deep bond with the environment. Native Americans clearly identified with the natural world and learned how to adapt to the climate, vegetation and wildlife. For thousands of years, they lived in and traveled across the Appalachian region, making their home a changing place from season to season. They killed wild game and grew crops for what they had to have for sustenance. Profit was not a part of their way of life. They searched for a balance between the natural world and man.

The Blue Ridge Mountains were mystical to not only the settlers but also the Native people. The misty blue haze that often wraps the tree-covered mountains gives rise to the name often afforded to that part of Appalachia. Those high mountains have their origin as sediments that were deposited in the seas and oceans that swirled around the drifting continents many hundreds of million years ago. Most of these sediments were sand, silt and clay particles that were washed down into the seas by rivers and streams that were eroding the continental landmasses of that time.

As I stand on the highest mountain in Tennessee, Clingmans Dome, I look westward and see the landscape below me. From 6,643 feet in elevation, most of the land we call Appalachia is beneath the elevation of Clingmans Dome and beckons the visitor, explorer, settler and seeker to come to this enchanted land.

The high mountains of the Blue Ridge reveal the erosive history that these mountain rocks have endured over the ages. Sweeping mountain ridges slope downward into the valleys below where eroded rock sediments floor the lowlands with fertile soil. The many high mountain tops and ridgelines give way to the lower foothills that border the Blue Ridge.

Native Americans as well as early European settlers found their place in the low coves and valleys where game could be hunted and crops grown. This untamed land quickly became the destination of an ever-searching people who were hardworking souls and full of a willingness to do what needed to be done to make a home, community and family.

As I look westward from Clingmans Dome high in the Great Smoky Mountains, the foothills quickly give way to a landscape totally unlike that of the high Blue Ridge region. Parallel ridges and valleys texture the great valley of East Tennessee as streams and rivers flow down between them. The rocks that underlie the long ridges and valleys owe their origin to sea sediments as well.

This ridge and valley area is tamer than the high Blue Ridge and afforded more opportunities for settlement. Larger valley floors provided more area for planting fields that were easier to cultivate and eventually pasture for the farms that were to develop in this land. Beautiful rivers coursed their way between ridges and over valleys.

The ridges in this washboard topography tend to be underlain by more resistant rocks like sandstone, siltstone and siliceous and cherty limestone and dolostone while the valleys tend to be underlain by less resistant strata like shale and shaley-limestone. The erosive power of the groundwater also left its mark as the soluble rocks like limestone and dolostone developed many cavities and caves with a surface topography pockmarked with sinkholes. Some of the more beautiful subsurface environments include places like Tuckaleechee Caverns, Bristol Caverns, and lesser-known caves such as Indian Cave, Cuyler Cave and Morrell Cave.

Progressing westward from the great valley of ridges and valleys, one abruptly encounters an upland characterized by massive sandstone rock strata, dark shale and deposits of coal. These mostly horizontal rock deposits resulted from the last few millions of years before the continents finally closed the shallow seas forming the great continent of Pangea. These rocks were the result of sediments formed by barrier islands, swampy lagoons, tidal channels, sandy beaches and intertidal zones of water and life.

Quartz pebbles and gravels, eroded from the closing landmasses, texture some of the sand deposits, which later would form conglomerates and conglomeratic sandstones. The barrier islands formed massive beds of cross-bedded sandstone, and the lagoons were the origin of the gray and dark shale. Some of the swampy environs would end up as coal deposits, some as thick as five to six feet.

As a result of the hard, resistant nature of the sandstone and conglomeratic sandstone, weathering of these strata has resulted in the formation of a tabletop plateau capped by these resistant rocks. Standing some 800 to 1,000 feet above the adjacent valley and ridge area, the Cumberland Plateau harbors an interesting and varied landscape, characterized by numerous waterfalls, canyons, rock shelters and overhangs and rock arches. At 256 feet in height, Fall Creek Falls, located on the Cumberland Plateau, forms one of the highest waterfalls in the eastern United States. These labyrinths of natural features characterize the tableland that we call the Cumberland Plateau and Appalachia Plateaus of several other states.

Settlers migrating westward from the ridges and valleys quickly found a resource that would change the country's energy future: coal. The high plateau land harbored coal deposits that were sandwiched between the sandstone layers and shale deposits. Undoubtedly, the Native Americans found some of these deposits earlier, before the white settlers moved into their lands.

The early pioneers used the coal not only for generating heat from burning the coal but also discovered that they could use coal to aid in their production of iron, later used for plows and guns. Along with the limestone and iron ore deposits found in the adjacent valley and ridge topography (limestone used for a flux) and coal for heating the iron ore, the settlers managed to produce abundant iron.

The Appalachian region that stretches from northern Alabama through Tennessee, West Virginia, Virginia and on into Pennsylvania would, in time, develop into a productive part of America. This region was a wild and rugged land in the early days of this country. But the settlers transformed some of the edges of the ruggedness into a more hospitable place: a place where settlements have grown into towns and cities, where wild rivers have been dammed, where trails and animal paths have been replaced by a complex network of highways, rail lines and trucking routes.

The vestiges of life shaped by the Native Americans and the early settlers are fast disappearing. Their settlements, homes and farms are being converted into subdivisions, golf courses, shopping districts and industrial regions. The rusted hulks of early farm machinery, automobiles and trucks and decaying homesteads are all that is left of most of these cultural artifacts. An entire generation of people is coming of age who will not understand what it took to build this country, the hard work, steadfastness and industriousness that formed the character of the early people.

The remnants of the culture that helped to shape our lives today are quickly waning as buildings are left in disrepair to rot and collapse and the implements of our agricultural history rust and decay into meaningless shapes. Old one- and two-room schoolhouses, churches and community general stores are becoming a thing of the past as our society blindly succumbs to the technology we create to make our lives seemingly easier and quicker paced.

How disappointed our ancestors must be in our rush to "better things" and an easier life. On our way to those ends, we leave a wake that has quickly pushed the things of that previous culture away to be forgotten and unappreciated.

2
MOUNTAIN FOLKS

The Appalachian Mountains, from the Blue Ridge and across the Cumberland Plateau, beckoned to the adventurous explorer, one who was willing to live off the land, withstand hardships, endure the environment and make do with what they had to survive. Those early settlers of the region were industrious and hard. If they didn't have what they needed, then they would just make it and go on with their business. Most knew how to scratch out a living, growing their own food and sustaining life. Some went a bit further to hone their skills, making such things as baskets, guns, pottery and fabrics.

Finding examples of these rugged individuals today is quite a task, as most have passed on, leaving their third and fourth generations who have moved up into the eighties and nineties of age. The authors found some such authentic individuals who remember their parents' and grandparents' way of life in the late nineteenth and early twentieth centuries. As these individuals progress onward, they take with them a fortune in history and culture that will never be replaced. Our effort was to capture some of these memories of life here in our section of Appalachia and what those memories compare to today and how their life has changed over time.

The following are some of the accounts we were able to capture from people who grew up in the mountains and remember those special times in our culture and how their way of life has changed. The hollows, coves, ridges and valleys brought shelter and fertile land for those brave folks willing to live in the mountains. This is their story.

Above: The mother of an unknown mountain family washes her children in a tub on the back porch. *Courtesy of the Tennessee State Library and Archives.*

Left: Wiley Gibson, a gunsmith from White Oak Flats (Gatlinburg today), holds one of his guns in this undated photo. *Courtesy of the Tennessee State Library and Archives.*

GREENBRIER

For humans to have a responsible relationship to the world, they must imagine their places in it. To have a place, to live and belong in a place, to live from a place without destroying it, we must imagine it. By imagination we see it illuminated by its own unique character and by our love for it.

—"It All Turns on Affection," by Wendell E. Berry,
from his 2012 Jefferson Lecture at the National Endowment for the Humanities

Glenn Cardwell

"Neighbors helped neighbors," said the late Glenn Cardwell, former mayor of Pittman Center, a beautiful vintage village in Emert's Cove on the edge of the GSMNP. Cardwell was born in Greenbrier Cove in 1930 along the banks of Indian Creek.

This was a different time, barely recognizable today, if at all.

Language use was quaint, said Cardwell, who retired in 1995 from the National Park Service after working as a naturalist interpreter for thirty-four years.

He recalled some "sayings" of his growing-up years:

"Soon it'll be 'dewing' time," meaning when dew would form in the evening.
"Shank of the day" was the end of the day.
"I rode on the shank of the mule," translated to the back end of the mule.
"Woods colt," he explained, meant a "bastard."
"Red Lane" was interpreted to mean a person's mouth and throat. It could be used in a sentence: "Watch what goes down the red lane."
"A decent howdy-do" was a nice hello, as in, "I can't get a decent howdy-do out of nobody."
One he heard often: "Today's preparation determines tomorrow's destination."

Cardwell's family, like many of the early Europeans who arrived within the boundaries of what is now the GSMNP, was of Scots-Irish heritage. They settled in the mountains that most resembled the land they left behind in Scotland and Ireland. Cardwell's father, Bill Cardwell, planted crops by the "signs," or using the moon phases to plant specific crops.

The late Glenn Cardwell (eighty-four at the time of this photo) of Pitman Center in Sevier County was born and raised in the Greenbrier section of the Great Smoky Mountains National Park and remembers the introduction of electricity, indoor plumbing and paved roads in that area of Sevier County. He later became a naturalist for the park, where he worked for thirty-four years; a younger Glenn Cardwell is pictured behind on the wall.

Bill Cardwell also recognized natural signs of woods lore. He knew to pick huckleberries when cicadas began singing, and he planted his corn when oak leaves got as big as a "squirrel's ear."

He placed root crops in a cellar, which was in front of the fireplace but in the floor. The family usually purchased only salt and sugar at a store. Everything else came from the farm, including honey to sweeten things.

Sorghum production was a community effort. The sorghum mill was owned by the community, and families shared. Everyone had a job during sorghum season.

Hollow black gum trees were used to make bee gums (a hive box, or a hive for bees). A bee gum's dimensions were normally a three-foot-long by a two-foot-diameter section of trunk for a bee gum. A flat piece of board was placed on top and bottom of the bee gum. Sticks covered in bees were placed inside the bee gum.

Many old-timers enjoyed eating the honeycomb, which was removed with the sticks used to plant the bees inside the bee gum in the beginning. Sourwood honey was a favorite in July.

Still others who have passed on now recalled the days when Cades Cove and farm fences were all split rail, and all of the split rails were cut from American chestnut trees.

One former Cove resident told writer Fred Brown, who reported it in a 1993 feature story in the *Knoxville News-Sentinel*, that he remembered "seeing them [chestnut trees]. Lord, they were everywhere. But about 1928, they disappeared. These woods then looked like a deer's head. They was all white like antlers."

People knew how "to do" then. Calico dresses had lined yokes, done by hand. Sleeves and necks were sewn with needle pleats. Times were thin, and many farm families were forced to put a patch on an already patched pair of overalls.

Sickness, as Glenn Cardwell said, was usually taken care of with some powerful potion from surrounding forest made of boneset or spice wood herbs. People ate wild mustard greens and "branch lettuce," which was found along "cold branches," to help stomach ailments.

Many of the oldest Cove residents told author Brown that when they had to leave their homes to make way for the Great Smoky Mountains National Park, it was "the end times."

That passing era is quickly leaving the modern world as well.

Think of the last time you witnessed a farmer plowing with a mule or even milking a cow by hand in the cool of a morning or late in the evening, walking along a split rail fence made of chestnut and watching as it fades away around a woods line curving along a dirt road.

This old cemetery resists the ravages of time in the Greenbrier area of the Smokies.

Cantilever barns were once common in the Appalachian region. The Great Smoky Mountains National Park has preserved a number of these old barns, like this one in the Greenbrier section of the park.

End times, the fading of a way of life, began eroding rural Appalachia after World War II. The displacement of land and people ramped up with progress, removing scenic vistas and heritage lands, the hooks and faults, short valleys and sweeping hillsides, so treasured by the first restless clans who were undaunted by the vast, raw wilderness of upper East Tennessee.

Today, there is little left of that precious picture, when the land and its people seemed at peace with themselves. Change has taken place in this beautiful land.

CADES COVE

Cades Cove in the Great Smoky Mountains National Park is a place of the heart, where sounds of another time reverberate from the forests, the fields and ancient stone hearths, where home fires were extinguished long ago. These sounds haunt our senses and tell us of another time and place and what we have so tragically lost in the presence of preservation.

Sounds of old souls rise from the sod in the Great Smoky Mountains National Park, like mist rising over streams and sailing into high ridges. Life in the park before it became GSMNP in 1934 was, perhaps, a microcosm of life just on the edges of the great land known as Appalachia.

Life was hard but abundant inside and outside the thousands of acres in Eastern Tennessee and North Carolina, which shared portions of a seemingly boundless river of earth. Forests were lush before logging trains arrived, and fields seemingly grew anything.

Inez Adams

Can you imagine? We can actually touch the logs that were touched by our ancestors.
—Inez Adams

When Inez "Granny" McCauley Adams died on February 8, 2016, one of the most gracious old souls left us. Like her mother, Dulcie Abbott McCauley, Inez documented her life in Cades Cove with a camera and by collecting photos from the past in the Great Smoky Mountains National Park.

Inez's passion was the history of her home place and its many generations of Appalachians. Her husband of sixty-plus years, Earl, was just as fervent and helped Inez with his amazing ability to dowse (using L-shaped coat hanger wires as his dowsing rods) the Cove and other areas inside the park for ancestral home sites, some dating to the nineteenth century.

Dulcie Abbott McCauley used a Kodak camera to photograph her life in the Cove. She was born in 1896 to John and Rhoda Lawson Abbott. Inez was born in Cades Cove to Millard and Dulcie Abbott McCauley in 1926. The family remained in the Cove until Inez was eight years old, when they moved away during the time the National Park Service began removing families, making way for the Great Smoky Mountains National Park.

Inez's grandparents were John and Rutha Myers McCauley and John and Rhoda Lawson Abbott. Her extended Cades Cove roots include Dan Lawson, Peter Cable and John Oliver, the first permanent white settler in Cades Cove. That is about as rich a Cove heritage as one can have.

From about 1915 until 1920, Dulcie Abbott snapped photos of the Cove and its people with her Kodak, a typical box camera of the era, such as the box Brownie.

Dulcie's eye and aim, however, were particular. She photographed people, mostly. However, hovering in the background of many of her photos are the old buildings of the Cove, there since the earliest of times when Cove life was a daily refrain of hard work in one of the world's most beautiful settings.

Above: Inez Adams as a child at her Cades Cove home in the early twentieth century. *Courtesy of Inez Adams.*

Left: Inez Adams as a young adult. *Courtesy of Inez Adams.*

By the time Dulcie was a teenager, her family had moved closer to be with her ailing grandparents. She was given a camera then and began examining the Cove through her simple lens. Inez once said she believed her mother may have gotten the camera by ordering it through a Sears catalogue.

Dulcie and her brothers, Luther and S.E. "Slick" Abbott, built a darkroom in one room of the Dan Lawson home, where she developed her black-and-white film. Dulcie's brothers also helped her in processing the film.

Just what that process was has been lost, Inez once said. She never did ask her mother how she was able to process the negatives and then print the film in the tiny darkroom in a corner of the Lawson home, with neither running water nor electricity.

Dulcie took hundreds of photos before she and her family moved out of the Cove in 1934, one of the last families to depart the gentleness of the Cove's languid landscape. Dulcie died in 1984, taking with her the secret of how she was able to work the film using no electricity and water from a spring branch. "I let her die without finding out," Inez told the author.

But Dulcie's daughter did not let the old photographs fade away. She copied more than three hundred of those photographs by her mother of early Cove life. They are, in a word, priceless.

There are snapshots of the old home places and photos of picnickers at Spence Field in Sunday finery. There are pictures of many families in the Cove, a precious history, which Inez used to create a large wall map depicting the home places in the Cove.

Also, Inez took her mother's legacy up another level. Where there were gaps in the collection, Inez obtained permission from the National Park Service to copy NPS files of Cove photos by park service anthropologists in the 1930s before the families were removed and before many of the early structures were either torn down or fell in.

And people in the area supplied Inez with family photo albums, which she copied to her collection. Inez did not stop with Cades Cove. She copied photographs of large areas of East Tennessee and its many families who shared photos with her.

In 1983, Inez purchased a used darkroom and equipment for about eighty-three dollars. Her husband, the late Earl M. Adams, designed a rig for a copying camera and accompanied Inez on their many jaunts looking for and copying photos.

The Inez Adams collection, held by family members, is a pictorial history, including some rare shots of the Cove, Townsend and Walland in a time that has all but disappeared. Not much is left of those days, except the remnants of old barns listing in a field or the crumbling skeleton of a stone chimney.

Why did Inez and Earl spend their "retirement years" capturing a time that has passed into the ages?

"There is an old story about the Primitive Baptist Church in the Cove," she explained once to the author.

> *A long time ago, there was a split in the congregation. Old-timers told me the differences were so great that it split the floor in the church. If you know where to look, you can see that the floor of the church did split at one time.*

> *Because there was a split in the membership, there was a split in the church. One day when I was there at the church, I also looked up to the rafters. I saw old handprints in the wood. I told a park ranger about it, who had never seen the handprints either. There they were, from all that long ago.*

Just as the handprints have been preserved, telling of the toil it took to build a church, so did Inez Adams preserve a prized past before it fell over the edge of time.

Mary Gene Roberts

Mary Gene Roberts's life reads like a chapter from the television series *The Waltons*.

Mary Gene Roberts discusses her life in the mountains of East Tennessee with the authors.

She was born in 1926 in a cottage by the schoolhouse in Sevier County. Her parents, Melvin E. and Ethel Swindler Lawson, were both teachers in Wears Valley. Melvin was the son of Richard West and Mary M. Lawson of Wears Valley. Melvin's grandparents once lived in Cades Cove in the Great Smoky Mountains National Park. Their home was located where the Cove campground and store are now.

Melvin graduated from Walland High School and promptly went off to World War II. After returning home, he graduated in 1950 from Maryville College. He then went to work at Alcoa Aluminum Company, in Maryville.

Mary Gene's family moved from Wears Valley to Maryville when she was three years old. She met her husband, Charles W. Roberts, at Maryville College in the mid-1940s. She graduated and became a registered dietitian.

Some of her earliest childhood memories center on visits to her grandparents' home in Wears Valley. She wrote about those memories in a detailed account for her family, used here with permission:

> *A fun memory was in going to the mill (the Old Mill in Pigeon Forge) to have corn ground into meal. Grandpa and I would shuck dried corn from the crib, shell it with a mechanical sheller and load it in a bran sack. Grandpa would*

saddle "Old Frank"; we would mount the horse with our corn and head for the mill. We waited for the corn to be ground and Grandpa purchased needed items at the local store. I would beg for a penny's worth of candy...usually successfully! It was also fun to build a "Go-cart" used to slide down a steep hill...the ruts were mud, kept muddy by adding lots of water to the ruts. The wheels were cross cuts from tree trunks.

Memories from that lifestyle are ever fresh. She wrote extensively. There were

nightly readings of the Bible by lamp light and getting old enough to read the devotion. The fun experiences of sharing in the daily work of feeding chickens, especially the bitties, gathering eggs, getting food from the dugout and its coolness, earthy odor and dirt walls. Apples were wrapped in newspaper stored in barrels. Hog killing time, cured meats in the smokehouse, milking the cows and trying to squirt fresh milk into the cats' mouths, playing in the creek and on wash day poking the clothes as they boiled in the old iron pot.

There were days of

hunting Indian arrow heads in the fields, hoeing corn, huge cooking time when the thrashers came, washing hands in the wash-pan and throwing the water onto the Elephant Ears plant. Blackberry picking, chiggers and briars, climbing up on the food safe for a snack and it almost turning over on me, straw ticks and feather beds, ironing with irons heated in the fireplace, trying to drive up the slick muddy hill to get to the farm. Dad would put on chains and Mother who did not drive, steered while Dad got out and pushed the car. At times we just had to leave it and walk; and with these memories, the undergirding of family love.

The muddy road was quite the adventure to Wears Valley in the 1930s. The Plymouth coupe struggled up mud-slickened hills. Their dog, Waggs, was a constant companion. But when her father purchased a new car, a 1938 Ford with two seats, Waggs was not familiar with the new vehicle's seating arrangement. He jumped in as if it were the old car and landed between the seats.

Mary Gene says she first drove a car at age eleven in Wears Valley when they visited her grandparents. Changing gears using a clutch was not always easy, she admitted. She would often "rake" the gears.

Left: Mary Gene Roberts's parents started the second motel to be established in Pigeon Forge, Tennessee. This photo shows the bedpost and footboard of one of the original beds in that motel.

Below: This postcard advertises Lawson Lodge, owned and operated by Mary Gene's parents in Pigeon Forge, Tennessee. Built and opened in 1940, the motel boasted private baths, home-cooked meals and reasonable rates. *Courtesy of Mary Gene Roberts.*

This 1919 photo shows Native Americans at the Dewight Indian Training School, located in Marble City, Oklahoma. Mary Gene's mother worked at the reservation school before returning to Tennessee and marrying. *Courtesy of Mary Gene Roberts.*

She recalled Pigeon Forge with only three stores and a post office located in the general store. Mildred Ogle was the postmistress. The old mail sorting table is now with Roberts's daughter.

In 1940, her parents built the second motel in Pigeon Forge, Lawson's Lodge. The motel was next door to the First Methodist Church. Even though it was named Lawson's Lodge, it had cabins.

Her father went to an antique store and bought the furniture for the motel. She remembered that he bought a bed for the hotel, and she still has it. The family sold the motel in 1949.

Prior to opening the lodge in Pigeon Forge, her parents ran the old Wonderland Hotel in Elkmont in the GSMNP one summer (1929 or 1930). She can remember running on the old porch outside with the rocking chairs.

Other memories that come to mind are harp singing in Wears Valley at the old Hedrick Chapel. She once owned an old song book with the harp notes in it.

Mary Gene recalled when the Little River would freeze over in Pigeon Forge and kids would go out on the ice and build fires. Some even drove an old car out on the ice to see if it held up. When the river flooded, she said, they would see outhouses, lumber and trees floating down the river.

She remembered that when she was young, the kids played games like Red Rover, pick-up-handkerchief and marbles. They would go home to eat lunch and then go back to school. Some children brought their lunches, since there was no lunch program then. When she lived in Sevierville, she bought a bicycle for two dollars and rode it in downtown Sevierville, which was dangerous due to all the traffic.

Families built "dugouts" into the sides of hills. Here they put their canned goods for storage on built-in shelves. A door usually covered the opening. Government regulations, she said, made families replace glass jars with metal cans. They also built springhouses over springs to keep dairy products cool.

Another memory is of her mother traveling to Oklahoma to work on the Indian reservation before she married her father. The Dewight Indian Training School was in Marble City, Oklahoma. Her mother returned home with a 1919 photo of one of the Indian families at the school.

Her parents are buried in Maddox Cemetery in Wears Valley; her father's family and the Walker sisters of Greenbrier are also buried there.

Lois Shuler Caughron

As you travel through Cades Cove in the Great Smoky Mountains National Park today, you are witness to a once-prevalent way of life that has vanished. Preserved log homes sprout here and there, saved by the National Park Service to offer a glimpse into another era. Wood-sided churches with louvered steeples and belfries where bells tolled church worship, births and deaths loom up, white and splendid on the side of a road or down a winding path. Ancient, encrusted tombstones stand watch in a churchyard. Some lean with age. There are no new stones here.

Lois Shuler Caughron lived in Cades Cove and recalls her times there as a child.

Lois Shuler Caughron, the last permanent resident to leave Cades Cove, recalled the essence of life in the Cove of eighty to one hundred years ago, a time so different from today that it is as if looking at a strange, out-of-focus scene. Although she was not born in the Cove, she moved there with her family at age one and then married a man who was born in the Cove.

Lois, eighty-six years old at the time of this interview, was born in Calderwood, Tennessee, where her father worked logging timber. The

This is the home place of Lois Caughron in Cades Cove. Her father was a Shuler and farmed in the cove. *Courtesy of Lois Caughron.*

family's home, however, was in Cades Cove, and they returned there in 1925, one year after Lois was born.

She attended the Consolidated School in the Cove, which was near the Primitive Baptist Church. The four-room school had an upstairs gym and two teachers. She went through the third grade there.

Her family had to move out of Cades Cove in 1936 along with many other families due to the formation of the National Park. This was a time of great upheaval and stress for families, who were oriented to the land in a way that is hard for us to understand today.

Lois's family moved to nearby Dry Valley near Townsend but later returned to the Cove for another short while. Another move sent the family to the Hubbard Community in Blount County, which contains most of the Great Smoky Mountains National Park within its county borders. Then, finally, Lois and her family returned to the Cove in 1942, when they found out that Kermit's father owned land in the Cove prior to the park giving them rights to live there.

She left the Cove permanently in 1999 after her husband of more than fifty-seven years, Kermit Caughron, died. Kermit was born in 1912 along Whistling Branch in the Cove and was eighty-six years old when he died. Lois and Kermit had four children, eight grandchildren, twenty great-grandchildren and two great-great-grandchildren.

Lois Caughron's father, Mr. Shuler, works the garden at his Cades Cove home prior to the establishment of the Great Smoky Mountains National Park. *Courtesy of Lois Caughron.*

Kermit and Lois raised cattle in the Cove until 1999. After Kermit died, the NPS told Lois she would have to remove the cattle from the 880 acres they owned inside the Cove. They had an agreement with the NPS concerning the land and their home. They were allowed to keep their cattle there in the Cove to help keep the grass eaten, which helped the park service maintain the "scenic beauty" in the vast cove lands across from their home. They called it "cleaned down."

Lois said that if you owned land in the Cove before the GSMNP was established, then you could lease that land back from the NPS. After she left in 1999, that program was ended; Lois was the last.

Their home was the old Dan Lawson house, which was built from the lumber and logs from the old Cable School house in the Cove. All four of their children were born and raised in the Cove. The house was on the south side of the Cove near the intersection of Hyatt Lane and the Cove road. In addition to raising cattle, Kermit and Lois put in a vegetable garden and raised bees for honey. Kermit set up several of those familiar box-like

Wood-burning cookstove in the Cades Cove home of Lois and Kermit Caughron. *Courtesy of Lois Caughron.*

Lois Caughron and her husband, Kermit, were known for their honey, which they sold to the visitors of Cades Cove. Shown here are Kermit and their son with jars of honey they sold at their Hyatt Lane home. *Courtesy of Lois Caughron.*

beehives near the road and fence in front of the house. Tourists often stopped and purchased fresh honey from him.

They had no electricity in the Cove, which meant cooking and heating was by wood. It was hard work keeping enough wood for cooking and heating, but Lois said the old woodstove also kept the house warm in the winter and hot in the summer.

She and Kermit eventually bought a generator to use with a washing machine. Prior to getting the washing machine, Lois washed clothes once a week at the nearby creek. An iron kettle was left permanently alongside the creek in which she would build a fire and heat wash water.

Their first electric washer, a Maytag, was purchased during World War II. It was the wringer roller type. Chuckling at the memory, Lois said her daughter kept getting her hand stuck in the wringer. Lois laughs today when she hears people complaining about having to wash clothes in fancy washers and then drying them out in big dryers.

Electricity neither provided light in her house nor ran any appliances. She had the electric generator she used for washing clothes only until she left the park in 1999.

Cooking on the woodstove, she said, kept the kitchen hot. She also ironed clothes in the kitchen using a flat iron she heated on the stove. Her husband, Kermit, would "bust" wood for use in the woodstove. Kermit said he busted wood during the day so he could sleep all night long.

When someone died in the Cove, the church they attended would toll the bell. Each church had a distinct-sounding bell for their church, so that people in the Cove knew immediately which church the deceased attended. The bell tolled the number of years for the deceased person's age. The bell, she said, did not "ding dong," which they knew as "ringing the bell." In death, the bell rang but once for each year, and that was known as tolling the bell.

When they were young, they attended the Primitive Baptist Church, where Lois's family is buried. They also attended the Missionary Baptist Church at one time. In addition to a piano and organ, the Primitive Baptist Church held harp singing once a year.

Three general merchandise stores—Hills, Birchfield's and Gregory's—served Cades Cove, Lois said.

She said the biggest positive change in her life was the arrival of electricity. Tourism and the hordes of tourists was the worst change she experienced. A constant stream of tourists interrupted their family life and work on the farm.

Pictured here is one of the Cades Cove families moving their belongings from the Cove home back in the 1930s. The Caughrons helped several families pack up for the move. *Courtesy of Lois Caughron.*

"Cove life," Lois said, "was not easy at all, even though it appeared to the outside world as being idyllic." Many daily chores required constant attention, such as carrying potable water from a nearby spring. They had to remove ashes from the woodstove daily. She canned food in the hot kitchen. In fact, the house was always hot, with no way to cool it.

Her children required constant care. And when one became sick, they had to travel to Maryville, Tennessee, for a doctor. She and Kermit did not use old family remedies.

Everybody in the family had a job to do, she said. Farm life was a dawn-to-dusk routine, often extending into the night beneath the stars or in bad weather.

There were rewards, such as sitting on a wooden porch in the cool of a night, listening to lowing cattle. A canopy of a star-lit sky enforced faith in a larger world. Night sounds of birds roosting and smaller critters scurrying about filled thoughts of other times and places. The curl of smoke from a distant chimney in winter spoke of a simple life lived in simpler times.

JOHN CLABO AND WEARS VALLEY

A portion of this section appeared in a 1994 edition of the Knoxville News-Sentinel.

John Clabo, who sat for this interview when he was ninety-five years old, last heard his favorite music when the mountains surrounding his home sang not with voices but with the baying of foxhounds.

In that time, red foxes, sly devils of the ridges, were plentiful. In spring, ravens blackened the skies and nested like bats in holes in the face of the mountain above his home. The birds were so plentiful old-timers named the mountain Raven Den.

Clabo, a thoughtful man who felt winter rhythms and summer dances of his mountains in Wears Valley where he spent most of his lifetime, speaks with an endurance found only in the mountains of Appalachia. His roughness and strength of character bring out an enduring quality that beckons for more information.

He grew up in Wears Valley in Sevier County and watched as the historic valley changed from tender placid beauty to swirls of traffic, rental cabins, helicopter flybys, people bristling to buy land as if it were on the shelf in a store sale.

The valley draws its name from Revolutionary War veteran Samuel Wear. He built a fort near the road from Pigeon Forge leading to Wears Valley. Other early names in the valley included Headrick, Clabo, Ogle and Brickey.

In his youth, John Clabo spent some nights on the mountains listening to the baying of his Walker Hounds as they scooted across the ridges and rammed down the ravines. The hounds cut into the draws chasing the flashing red fox, as wily a creature as could be found in the woods.

There was a special elixir in those nights and the music of the hounds on the hunt, skedaddling across mountains known as Pine, Sinkhole, the Hogback, Big and Little Rocky.

"I'd rather hear them dogs than regular music," said the man who once played traditional mountain music with his brothers and sisters in homes that dotted the valley. He did not see much difference in the art of training hounds to sing into the hills as they flung themselves like fury into the black mountain nights.

John Oliver Clabo was a link to the nineteenth century, to the War Between the States and a precious history of Wears Valley. That history is fading under development and the disappearance of farming.

In his youth, a time when the main road into Wears Valley was jaw-snapping mud and gravel, John Clabo worked with his father, brothers and sisters farming more than three hundred acres of sweet valley land. Here crops sprung up without need of insecticide. There were no bugs in gardens, which provided a gracious plenty.

He remembered his father, Archie, and uncle Sam Hammer Clabo, who purchased the farm in the early 1890s, hiring job-hungry people who walked across the mountains from Pigeon Forge.

The laborers worked on a kind of agricultural barter system: strong backs in the field in exchange for hams, flour and corn. That was a time of whippoorwill peas, fattening hogs that were not slaughtered until they reached 250 pounds on the hoof, two-horse hay rakes and hay in windrows.

"When neighbors saw you raking, they would grab up their rakes and come over to help." Those human roots feeding into the soil and spreading were close in the generations. His father told him stories about growing up in Pigeon Forge on Mill Creek in the crash-and-boom era of the Civil War.

"I used to go with my father to Pigeon Forge to take wheat. He showed me where he hid a yoke of oxen. He had to take them to Dry Pond Mountain and Pine Mountain to keep them hid from the soldiers."

His father also showed him where he buried a homemade fifty-bushel hogshead wooden barrel up to its wide mouth and filled it with the family's corn to keep it safe from starving soldiers in blue and gray. Later, that barrel moved with the family from Mill Creek to Wears Valley and was around in Clabo's youth.

He worked in Mascot zinc mines and then ventured into the coal towns of Kentucky, where he worked in deep drift mines for nineteen years.

Clabo met Sally Combs, who worked as a waitress in a boardinghouse in Wheelwright, Kentucky. He and Sally married in 1931. She died childless in 1986, leaving behind her husband of fifty-five years to live out his days wandering past the solid walnut four-poster bed, dresser, chair and chest of drawers he bought for Sally in 1936 for $300.

Clabo and Sally moved between coal camps in Kentucky, and at one point, they wound up in West Virginia. Eventually, in 1943, he stopped coal mining. "The night before I quit, I got a dread on my mind."

He had seen men crushed by slate and the hard and perilous hours under ground, cutting coal from dangerously hanging rock the miners nicknamed "horseback" and "kettle bottom" because of their shape and size. He worked in twenty-seven-inch coal seams, meaning he was forced

John Clabo moved from Wears Valley to work in the coal mines of Kentucky digging out beds of coal before moving back to Wears Valley. *Courtesy of Tennessee State Archives.*

to lean his head at an angle while on his knees, chopping black chunks for twelve dollars a day for eighteen hours of work.

The low coal and long hours took their toll on his mind and nerves. "I came out at 11:00 a.m. that morning. I was supposed to be back that afternoon at 3:00 p.m. But once I was out, I knew I wasn't going back. I was outside."

John Oliver Clabo came home to Wears Valley to farm again. He wanted to dig in the valley's good earth and feel its power that only a farmer can know on those special mornings when he arises and looks out over corn tassels glimmering in the morning sunlight, glinting with a beauty so pure it can hurt the heart.

Long before he left the valley, Clabo worked in what is now the Great Smoky Mountains National Park, hauling "acid" wood to a leather tanning operation in Townsend. He boarded with John Walker, father of eleven, including the five famed spinster Walker sisters, who lived in a 130-year-old cabin on Little Greenbrier Cove, where mountain meets morning in a translucent green rapture.

Clabo carried chestnut tree posts crosscut sawed by his brothers for the tannery. The bark was used to color the hides. "I hauled four loads of wood a day, two in the morning and two in the evening," Clabo said.

"I boarded with Uncle John Walker. Each one of those sisters had a particular job to do. One did the cooking. One milked the cows; one did the weaving."

Just like John Clabo, those days and seasons have faded and curled into the folds of time. He no longer coaxes ornery mules from off Little Greenbrier to Townsend.

John Clabo no longer hears the music of his foxhounds, scooting across the mountains circling Wears Valley where he walked steadfastly across the ridges. That could be because the fox population has dropped off. He was, arguably, the finest fox hunter in Appalachia due to his longevity, if not for sheer ability.

Subdivisions sprout now where once there was a lush valley of his youth. "We had a beautiful place here in this valley. It was practically all farmland. People farmed and lived off the land," he said.

He once knew everyone in the valley. At the time of this interview, he said he did not know one-third of the people. "I used to see everyone I knew in church." Back then you knew who everyone was. Today people are out to try to get anything you got. "I wish it were like it was. You could get on the mountains and you could let your dogs run. I always loved to hear my Ranger."

Apple orchards brimmed with horse apples, mare apples and sweet apples. From his back porch, he pointed a bent finger. "See that rose bush there," he said, directing his eyes toward a gathering of thorny rose stems, rising from a single source and fanning out at the top. "Those roses are over one hundred years old; Came here when my father and uncle Hammer bought this farm and moved in from Mill Creek. They are called red blaze. You can't find them anymore."

Like his once peaceful valley where the fox ran and the raven flew, you cannot find that anymore except in a perfect longing or surviving in old imagination and mountain memories.

3
APPALACHIAN LANGUAGE

The disappearance of Appalachian culture includes many material items such as farming implements, structures, furniture, clothing and food and medicinal practices, to name a few. Other things such as music, faith, traditions and speech are not as easy to examine. In particular is the Appalachian language, which is disintegrating as the influx of people into the region from other cultures increases. Pressure to change the old-fashioned way of speaking to a more modern accent and vocabulary also increases with the change in populations.

Harder still is the ability to capture this language in context to gain the feel of that spoken language. Most of the influx of people into Appalachia during the 1700s and 1800s was from Scotland, England and Ireland. According to Montgomery and Hall's *Dictionary of Smoky Mountain English*, the language of much of Appalachian English came from Ulster and Scotland, while the pronunciation has ties with southern England. Theorists used to propose that the Appalachian language was a throwback to Elizabethan English or Shakespearian English. However, academic researchers have largely discounted that idea.

It is not to say that certain words or phrases do not resemble or even come from the British Isles, it is that most of the Appalachian speech is thought to have originated within the Appalachian region from the English language that the early settlers brought with them.

With that said, the Appalachian accent and language is fast dissolving into a blend of many English forms. Only in the rural areas of Appalachia can

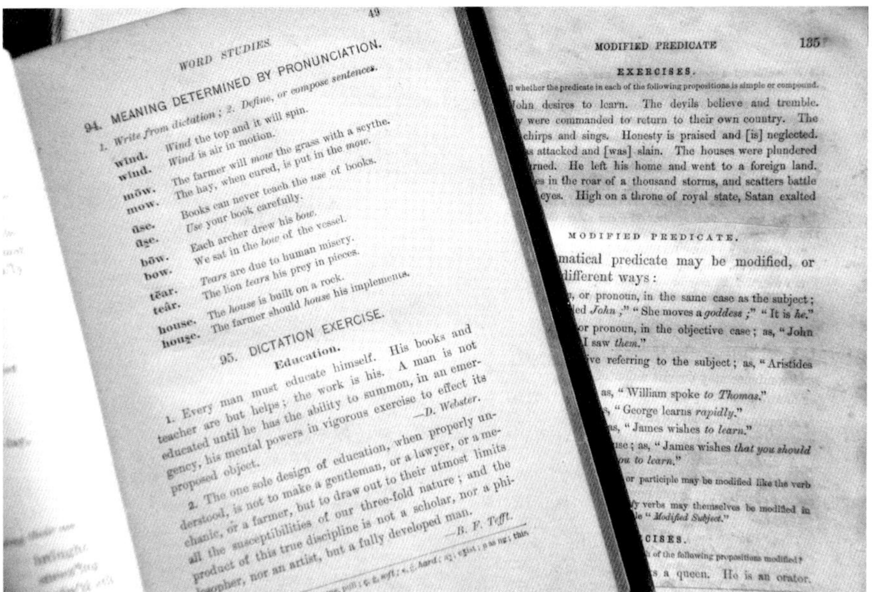

These old grammar books date from the nineteenth century and were found in rural Tennessee. Correct grammar and spelling were taught in all communities at the local schoolhouse.

one still hear the spoken language in an authentic accent. This language and spoken word have been passed down from generation to generation, as some inhabitants of the region can trace their ancestors back into the early 1700s.

City folk commonly mistake and ridicule the rural speak as a sign of low education and intelligence. However, much to the chagrin of the city folk, these people have retained a way of life and a work ethic second to none in the country. They often make things they do not have, invent things they need to do a chore or job and will work daylight to dark if need be to complete a task. Characteristics not often found in the urban setting.

Sometimes understanding a rural Appalachian local can be quite a task. Even those who are used to hearing the Appalachian speak can be confused at times as to what is being said. There are pockets of people that speak the "mountain talk" and do not think anything about it. An example of old Appalachian speak or "mountain talk" is given below:

> *My maw be from the holler betwixt Stone Peak and Log Ridge. Where her parents came from I don't rightly know. I do recall visitin up in em hollers and seen how they'uns lived. They was coons that crawled all over the place, and way back up the holler is a skull orchard, next to the chapel. I*

was afeared a many a time to mess with those fellers. I haint never heered of such doins as came out of that there holler. My maw and paw wernt larnt much, but they'uns woud have a hissy fit if we chillern were caught takin a chaw or sippin corn-juice.

My mee maw took sickly one year and paw had to do the chores for em. Me, I was fair to medlin most of the time, not much peaked, sorta stout. I wunst rode the shank of a onery mule neigh about five mile to get some store-boughten clothes. We'uns don't have much store clothes, so it was special. I'd carry them clothes in a poke so as to not soil them. Sometimes the poke was plumb full and a fit to carry.

I recollect tryn to get shed of an ole dog one day whilst visitin in the holler. You'uns wont believe what that animile done. Why he sure-enough took a notion and might near drank all of paws stump water. Why that ole dog took a shine to that corn-juice and stayed might near all night next to the still.

This here tow sack would keep varmints till we'uns could get'em out of the country. They law, one time ole dog chased a polecat up a bee gum. He barked and yelled all night, kept us'uns awake till the sun shined. We had to make backer juice to daub on that poor feller until the sting went away.

Yonder is where mee maw gets her yairbs to make poultices for when we get ivy all over us. She fixes vitles something else too. Best cornpone in the holler, I reckon; that and soup beans is somthin else.

Well, I better quit this here foolish talk and get on back to my chores. Looks like a gullywasher is a comin directly and it could get airish. I heard them jarflys and they make a right smart sound in the wood. I hope all my sayins meant something to you'uns. It soon be dewing time and the shank of the day is comin on.

Today, a person would be hard pressed to find someone who still talked this way. However, many of the words are still in use and can be heard in the rural parts of Appalachia. Words like *you'uns*, *backer*, *mater*, *airish*, *vitiles* and *right smart* are some examples. Other words that characterize the Appalachian speak include words that substitute "te" for "ght" in spelling and enunciation. These include such words as *brite* (for bright), *lite* (for light), *site* (for sight) and *mite* (for might).

Other parts of the Appalachian speak involve idioms or, as the Appalachian people say, sayings. These are short phrases or even words that express one's thoughts, feelings or actions. These include words like *mosey*, meaning to move slowly, or *skedaddle*, meaning "let's get out of here fast." Another short expression is the word *druthers*, which means "choice": I'd druther go to town as sit here all day! Or, if I had my druthers, it would be ham over liver.

Sometimes these sayings involve several words, as in "that boy ain't worth his salt," which means he is lazy or trifling. Another common expression used in the southern Appalachians is "carry you [me, them] someplace." This means in rural Appalachian speak to take someone or something to someplace. An example would be: "Will you carry me to town?" A more confusing phrase to non-Appalachian people is the saying: "I don't care to." This actually means that a person is willing to do what was suggested or said. "Will you carry me to town?" "I don't care to do that," means that they do not mind taking that person to town.

This manner of speaking is all but gone in the cities and urban areas but still exists in some of the more rural parts of Appalachia. More examples of these phrases include "we had a frog tickler of a rain last night" and "man, what a gully washer we had the other day," both meaning that there was a heavy rain. Another phrase that expresses someone being happy is "He's grinning like a opossum eatin' persimmons"; opossums are known to eat persimmons, which can be very bitter to the taste at times.

Another phrase commonly used in the Appalachian region is "He is hell-bent-for-leather," meaning that a person is determined to do something. An example of where one would use this phrase would be in describing a person who is working furiously, persistent and unending in a garden or some other endeavor.

When a person intends to do something, they "aim to" do it. The use of the word *aim* has several meanings and is used in the Appalachian region quite frequently; the meanings would include "to point" and also "intend." One comical but serious phrase that uses both meanings in the same sentence was found inside an outhouse in Sevier County. The phrase was inscribed on a board and hung over the "portal" and said: "We aim to please, you aim too, please!"

Another saying that involves how well a person can hear goes like this: "She can hear a mouse peeing on cotton." Think about that for a minute! What a descriptive phrase. Also, pertaining to something that won't work or won't do, the country folk would commonly say: "That dog won't hunt." And another phrase pertaining to dogs includes the following: "That is as crooked as a dog's hind leg." Even better is when something is not straight but proclaimed to be straight like a curvy road: "That road is as straight as a dog's hind leg."

One common saying used in rural Appalachia is "that person is slower than molasses," referring to how slow molasses flows out of a jar. Molasses is usually thick and viscous when being poured. When I was a child, I used to hear this saying a lot: "I'll light a fire under you," meaning if you don't do what I told you to do, I am going to spank you to get you going. We kind of knew what that meant when the adults told us that. In combination, a saying might go like this: "You are shucking that corn as slow as molasses and if you don't get going faster on that I'll light a fire under you!"

A few more sayings include the following: "slow as the day is long," "he's lost his marbles" and "the pot calling the kettle black." The saying "slow as the day is long" refers to long summer days, usually fifteen to eighteen hours long, and the phrase is usually a comment about how slow someone or some activity is moving. Another version of the saying is "you are slower than Christmas," meaning that Christmas takes a long time to get back around on the calendar. The common phrase "he's lost his marbles" refers to someone who may not be thinking straight, as in "he told us to walk across the street in traffic! Why he's lost his marbles if he thinks I'm going to do that!" The third saying, although not original to Appalachia, comes from Spain (Cervantes's *Don Quixote*), and is usually said about someone criticizing someone else for a feature they both share: "Boy, that's the pot calling the kettle black!" Both the pot and the kettle are the same color.

Research into the history of the Appalachian language has been sparse up until recent times. Although he has written widely on the linguistics of Southern Appalachia, Michael B. Montgomery produced a work that is the first of its kind—a *Dictionary of Smoky Mountain English*. Based on previous work by Joseph S. Hall, who signed on with the Park Service in 1937 to collect and record the language, music, folk medicine and beliefs of the people in the Great Smoky Mountains of Tennessee and North Carolina, Montgomery put together a monumental record of Appalachian speak.

In his research, Montgomery discovered that the language of Southern Appalachia is native and original, grew from its native Scotch-Irish roots, but sprouted anew in this Appalachian region. The language of the Southern highlands, he says, is neither Elizabethan, nor Shakespearean, as has been written, but is Southern Appalachian—from the mountains and uniquely ours.

Over time, Montgomery developed a network of consultants native to the mountains of Tennessee and North Carolina. Glenn Cardwell, former Great Smoky Mountains National Park ranger from Sevier County who grew up in the park before it was a park, and others were used to verify certain words and usages and to provide sources for quotations. Montgomery did not use a single quotation if he could not find the original source.

From 1994 through 1998, he worked with the ten consultants: Inez Adams of Blount County; Roy D. Brown of Cocke County; Florence Bush of Sevier County; Cardwell; Michael Ellis of Carter and Unicoi Counties; Loyal Jones of Cherokee and Clay Counties in North Carolina; Ted Ledford of Mitchell County, North Carolina; Pearl Norris of Cherokee County, North Carolina; Duane Oliver of Haywood County, North Carolina; and Jack Weaver of Ashe County, North Carolina.

"Essentially, this dictionary has attempted to distill the language from the vast collection of material that has been preserved and also from the minds of people who grew up in the mountain communities," Montgomery told the author.

"This is not so much a dictionary as it is an encyclopedia. And it is not just a dictionary, but a dictionary of Southern Appalachia. There is material on every subject under the sun when it comes to the mountain culture." Although the dictionary is of the Smoky Mountains, it covers a much broader area. Much of that area pertains to Southern Appalachia in general.

He said during this interview that the hardest work of all was defining a word. "Defining the terms was extraordinarily time-consuming and demanding. I had countless phone conversations with Glenn [Cardwell] and others to capture the nuance and define words. I had to define words in areas that I knew nothing about." For example, Montgomery said there are twelve to fifteen terms defining a mountain plow in mountain culture.

"There are quite a few terms in this dictionary that are new. At most 20 percent of the mountain language can be traced across the water (Atlantic Ocean). Some of that is new to America, newly coined here." Montgomery says there are hundreds of terms found only in Appalachia. It is obvious, he asserted, that they are new words and have no relevance to the old country.

The word *moonshine* has forty different related terms in the dictionary. *Mountain dew*, he believes, might be an Irish term, but *white lightning* is American.

Here are a few of the terms that are classified purely as Smoky Mountain English:

* ADDLE-PATED: (adj.) addled, dazed, confused, mentally weak or deficient.
* AGEABLE: (adj.) old, advanced in years.
* AGG, AGG UP: (v.) to egg on.
* ALLERS: (adv.) always.

* Angel biscuit: (n.) a buttermilk biscuit made from yeast dough, kneaded and left to rise before baking.
* Backjaw, back sass: (v.) to talk back, reply impertinently.
* Bark: (v.) to scrape, knock the skin off.
* Bell-tail: (n.) a rattlesnake.
* Biddy peck: (v.) to nag mildly.
* Cackleberry: (n.) a hen's egg.
* Cantdog man: (n.) a fellow who uses a short-handled peavey, or pole or a short lever with a sharp spike on the end and a hook on the side, used to maneuver a log on a skidway or in water.
* Careen: (v.) to lean or bend to one side.
* Cat: (n.) a rudimentary form of baseball played by children.
* Do-less: (adj.) lazy, dilatory, doing little, inefficient.
* Doomawhichit: (n.) a thing whose name is not recalled for the moment; also thing a majig
* Flander: (v.) to splinter, shatter, spill.
* Hogback ridge: (n.) a mountain ridge that slopes sharply on each side and often has jutting rocks, resembling the high, narrow back of a wild hog.
* Mommick: (n.) a state of disarray or confusion.
* Scotch: (v.) to place a rock or other object under a wheel to prevent it from moving to impede thwart.
* Scutter: (n.) a mischievous or mean-spirited person, rascal, scamp.
* Swag: (v.) to sag, sink down, bend in the middle as from overweight.
* Timber doodle: (n.) the pileated woodpecker.
* Toadskin: (n.) a dollar bill.
* Upscuddle: (n.) a quarrel.
* Yankee dime, Yankee nickel: (n.) a kiss, usually given to a child in return for a small favor such as doing a household chore.
* You'uns: (pron.) all of you.
* Zonies alive: (interj.) a mild oath.

And then, of course, there is southern speak, language from the southern flatlands, which is somewhat different from the Appalachian speak but often blended into a mix of the two in modern times. Those of us fortunate enough to live in the South, especially Appalachian Tennessee, often take our language for granted. We don't see anything very special about the way we talk. But there is.

To speak southern, you must learn to lengthen vowel sounds, add a little molasses, divide your words into halves and then into fourths. Next, you just drop the last syllable. It's not needed anyway. For example, we usually respond to our fathers and bosses as "Yes, suh" and "No, suh."

Other examples of southern speak include:

It is "ova theah" instead of "over there." As in, "You'll find the moonshine ova theah behind the wood box, but leave me some."

Tennessee is Tensea or Ten-o-sea. Georgia is Jawja. Alabama is not mentioned in polite company.

You ain't nothing but a "houn dawg" leaves off the D in hound, and dog is pronounced dawg.

Some other words and phrase definitions:

ALABAMA: Not a country and western band but the state which Ten-o-seans love to hate. Do not, repeat, do not shout "Roll Tide!" in Ten-o-sea. It could get you drawn and quartered.

BARBECUE: It is the regional food of choice and takes training to create. Recipes are handed down from one generation to the next, if they get around to it. Barbecue uses any of a variety of meats, from raccoon to billy goat.

BASS BOAT: A craft of mythical proportions for which good ol' boys will mortgage house, wife and children.

BLUE TICK: Does not refer to blue ticks but is a legendary breed of houn dawg, which one speaks of very reverently in front of the owner. For example, you might greet a fellow with a blue tick by saying something like: "Billy Joe Bob, I been wunnerin' 'bout yo houn. He's the best dawggone dawg I ever saw."

CATHEADS: Has nothing to do with fishing. Means cathead biscuits, which are cooked on wood-burning stoves. It is best to be quite complimentary about a cook's catheads. It is OK to say, "You got the best little catheads I ever tasted." But it is considered bad manners and could end up in a shooting or a cutting to refer to the cook's biscuits as "flat catheads."

CORNBREAD: A legendary pan food that is the first thing good ol' boys and good ol' girls eat when they are weaned from mother's milk. It will not have sugar in it, ever!

DINNER: Very large meal in the middle of the day.

DIXIE: Waitress at the Dew Drop Inn.

FRIED CHICKEN: An extremely fine food source of protein and vein-clogging cholesterol eaten with the fingers. Top of a southerner's food chain.

Goobers: A leguminous annual herb that is best put inside a Coke bottle and swigged while at the feed store or filling station with Bubba. Some people refer to them as peanuts. Can also be a person's name.

Grits: Pronounced gri-utts, should be the national food. Can be eaten by itself but is best mixed with sausage and eggs, bacon and eggs, cheese and eggs or gravy and eggs.

Hushpuppies: Does not refer to dog discipline. It is a cornpone concoction with onions and other secret ingredients that tastes almost as good as cornbread.

Mess: Has nothing to do with a state of a child's room or an emotional condition. A mess is quantity. As in, "I ate a mess of collards for dinner."

Moonshine: Is not a brightly lit night. Moonshine is a special southern elixir that sometimes causes grown men to howl at the moon like houn dawgs. After drinking this secret potion, some men have been known to wake up the next morning wondering how the family pickup wound up in the treetops.

Moonshiner: One who makes moonshine, usually deep in the woods where he can be alone to religiously meditate over the secret recipes that have been guarded and handed down over the ages.

Supper: Very large meal at night, normally centered on fried chicken or barbecued chicken or both.

Whar: Sounds like "war" but means a place you are going to or coming from. As in: "Whar you goin'?"

So, we stretch our words. Like a good sop of molasses. It may take us all day to get there, but like the sign says, "I may be slow, but I'm ahead of you." We are famous for losing our Rs and other consonants. In fact, some of us sound as if we are coming from where we have already been.

We are drawlers in the South. We like it like that. It is quite lyric to hear someone from South Carolina render a good morning, a Tennessean ask how you are doing of a day or a North Carolinian or a Virginian or a Georgian or an Alabamian say anything.

Our language and our dialect are precious cultural jewels, handed-down treasures to be protected. I suppose we need to be patient and understanding with those who are less tolerant. But it is hard to be humble when you are from the South. And it is difficult to become accustomed to hearing our language homogenized and disappearing like many a southern scene.

As time continues to march on, the influx of people from outside of Appalachia will continue to dilute and change the culture of most of its defining character points. Language is distinctive as it is spoken and written from different parts of the United States. This is especially true of the Appalachian region with its unique spoken language. In time, the language from the hills and valleys of Appalachia will be diluted to the point that our Appalachian language will be dissolved into a more pluralistic "all American" style. Accents, words, sayings and speaking styles are all a part of the Appalachian language culture and all contribute to the uniqueness of our Appalachian heritage. It is with this in mind that we acknowledge the distinctive nature of the Appalachian language and our responsibility to preserve it.

PART II

A PEOPLE AND THE LAND

4
ROBERT NICLEY

Living in the hollows of the rugged land of Appalachia were families who were as rugged as the land they settled. They raised their food, built their houses and barns and made whatever else they needed to subsist in the vast territory. Those early settlers became hardened to the cold winters and dry, hot summers. Some were stubborn and stayed put, while others moved onward, westward.

The late 1800s and early 1900s were especially hard on the folks of Appalachia, most barely subsisting; many succumbed to disease and illness but passed on to the next generation a way of life that has all but disappeared today. Some of those descendants, in their eighties and nineties at the time of this writing, remember the early days of the twentieth century and the change that has taken place in their lifetimes. Their willingness to talk about those times is a gift shared in this writing. The following stories are but a sampling of what Appalachian life was like in the early twentieth century.

Robert Nicley was eighty-six years old at the time of this interview. He is as thin as a cornstalk but strong as a spring storm. His face is craggy and lean, like his body, that looks as if it might snap in the middle. He wears work clothes because that defines him and his life. Work. Farm work. His hands are large, rough, chipped and scarred, but easy on the handshake. There is a moment of the rising sun in Robert Nicley's face as he greets you.

He grew up on a farm in Grainger County, raising beef cattle, chickens and anything else the family needed to survive. He worked from sunup to sundown and can keep those kinds of hours. A shed next to his farm home in

Left: Robert Nicley lives in Dutch Valley in northern Grainger County. He remembers when they first got electricity, which he said, "changed life for everyone." His mother's family moved to Dutch Valley in 1735.

Below: Looking out from Robert Nicley's home in Dutch Valley, one can see why solitude was a characteristic of rural life in Appalachia.

Dutch Valley is crammed wall to wall, floor to ceiling full of old farm tools. They still work.

He helped his father build hip-roof barns, a European-style barn with a sloping roof on all sides. A large barn of fifty-foot beams of hardened dead oak graced the family acreage, standing on a slight rise like a graying sentinel. Gray slabs of limestone lay here and there, mostly in a linear pattern along the base of the ridge.

Robert's grandfather was Sebastian "Boss" Nicley. He had a grocery store and 160 acres of land. Robert recalled from family stories that his great-grandfather James Nicley moved into Dutch Valley around 1916. He noted that the Nicleys were probably in Grainger County sometime before that, in the late 1800s.

There were many Nicleys, he said, and Nicelys. The difference in the spelling depended on a family's political leanings. Republicans spelled the name Nicley, and Democrats spelled it Nicely.

Robert inherited land from his mother, Ida Layel Beeler, who inherited it from her family, family land dating back to 1735 when John Valentine Beeler first arrived and settled on Williams Creek, just upstream from Beelers Mill. Williams Creek connects to what is now the Norris Lake watershed in the Black Fox community. In fact, Robert lives on a portion of the Beeler farm today and is the sixth or seventh generation to live there. The Beelers were "Black Dutch," meaning of German descent. Robert's grandfather (on his mother's side) was Robert Houston Beeler, a Civil War veteran, who was a blacksmith for the Union army.

Robert did not finish high school but did complete his GED and then had two years of college at Lincoln Memorial University near Harrogate, Tennessee. His family did not get electricity until 1948, a time he remembers vividly. When electricity arrived, it seemed like a marvel. The home had light, usually a single cord dropping from the ceiling like a black snake.

Before the Tennessee Valley Authority supplied the electricity, homes were very dark at night. And in that time, when it became dark, people, especially farm families in the rural areas, simply went to bed. Lights provided a different way of life. Families could now read together, especially the Bible. Next came radios, stoves and refrigerators.

Robert said it was easy to know if a family were home: lights would be on and easily seen.

Before the lights came on in rural Grainger County, life was anything but easy on country farms of the years during and after the Great Depression. Robert was twelve years old before he took his first trip to Knoxville, just a little over forty miles away. He had two pair of overalls, one for work and one for school.

Women washed clothes one day a week, done outside the house, usually in a black pot. The water was heated over an open fire. His mother eventually got a washing machine with a gas motor.

A simple bartering system was in place for communities and farm families. Robert carried eggs, lumber and other goods to a nearby store to barter

Left: Among other farm chores, Robert Nicley makes wood furniture like these rocking chairs shown here.

Below: This photo shows a portion of Robert Nicley's wood shop in Dutch Valley.

for staples the family needed, like coffee, sugar and salt. He also recalled desperate Depression hobos jumping from railroad trains, begging for food and asking to do chores for any kind of work.

The first tractor on the Nicley farm was a John Deer "H" 1937, with steel cleat wheels. Before the tractor arrived, Robert and his father plowed behind mules and horses.

The mule teams were used for the mean, hard work of dragging logs from forests. They called it "Beaver'en" logs, like "snaking" logs. In addition, his family owned a sawmill and planted tobacco, which paid for the farm's annual taxes.

One of Robert's jobs was to keep the kitchen wood box filled. Wood was used not only as heat but also fuel to cook on a wood stove. He made sure the wood box was full each evening. Saturday, he said, was wood-gathering day.

Water did not stream from a spigot on demand but from a fresh spring located about five hundred feet from the house. Milk, eggs, butter and cream were all submerged or lodged carefully in the spring to keep cool. Butter was supplied by churning milk into cream and cream into butter. Churning was done by hand in a large earthen or ceramic container. The wooden pole used was known as the dash.

Freshly prepared and slat sugar–cured hog meat would be hung in a smokehouse, normally a small barn-like structure. Most of the hog was cut into hams. On this, Robert and his father would cure the meat with salt or sugar and a seasoning paste. The hams were then wrapped in paper bags and then hung from the smokehouse rafters for about a year to cure.

Before eating, the meat was usually soaked in water to remove the salt. Then it was usually fried, and "leavings" in the skillet began what is known as "red-eye gravy." The gravy was normally poured over grits and fresh-cooked buttermilk biscuits.

Most hogs were killed on Thanksgiving Day, a day when most people were at home to celebrate. Before the big Thanksgiving feast, relatives and friends helped with the hog killing, which is pretty much a lost art today.

Robert said just about every piece of the hog was kept for eating: brains for chitterlings (intestine), bladder, tongue, ribs, hams and even the feet for pickling. An old country saying is that every part of the hog was used for food, except its "snort."

Robert laments that few people farm today. Most people do not know how to farm and indeed cannot even grow a garden. He shakes his head, wondering what people will do for food should another Great Depression arise, or worse.

Farming was a way of life in his youth. You farmed the land. It was all-day, hard work. That may be one reason why people work in crowded cities and think their groceries come from the big-box stores. Farming, Robert said, wore a body. "By the time a person was fifty years old, they were 'broke-down' from working so hard on the farm."

Other everyday life along those old country roads included the arrival of indoor plumbing. "Going to the old outhouse when it was twenty degrees and having to use a slick page from a Sears and Roebuck catalogue was not fun," Robert said. "Thin pages," he quipped, "were the best."

Women entertained themselves with "quilting bees." Most country houses had a quilting room in which the quilting frame hung from the ceiling, awaiting a gathering.

Robert's one-room school, Lay School, was near the Jake Lay and Austin Lay Store, known as a general store. Here farm and rural families bought coffee, sugar, salt, shoes, cloth for making clothes and farm tools. "Back then we used to say if you bought it right, you can sell it right." That meant if a farmer could buy an item cheaply, he would sell it later for a reduced price.

Robert pointed out that is no longer the way of things. The idea of a community, he believes, has disappeared. "People were more compassionate for their fellow man. They had trust for people. There were no locks on doors. That's not the same today. The sense of community is gone," he said

Other large changes include the value of goods and services. He recalled paying twenty-five cents for goods that cost five dollars today. Gas was five cents a gallon and today runs to almost three dollars or more.

Robert Nicley laughs about the times on the farm when he was a young boy. He lives in the valley that his ancestors settled in 1735.

Ambulance service was once operated by the local funeral home. Today, it is a separate service.

Crude oil was used to keep dust down on roads, stores and schools. A light coating of oil on wood floors reduced dust.

Church in Robert's youth was especially important. Entire families attended a single church or even started one. If a church member missed too many services, or committed some misdeed, they were "churched," meaning they were asked to leave the church.

Since most houses were not insulated, keeping warm in winter was a singular event. A large fireplace was usually central to the house. A large "stick" log or a "back log" kept embers burning all night. Those logs were commonly hickory or oak. And many a hand-stitched quilt piled up on beds to keep warm, along with heated bricks or rocks.

"People had common sense then. Today, common sense is hard to find. Back then we kept our hands and brains busy."

5
DAVID MITCHELL

What's time to a hog?

That line may seem frivolous or even part of a joke. It is not. It is from a farmer who has seen many hogs come and go. He has watched sunrises as he milked cows by the hundreds at his dairy farm. He has watched the sun set as he milked those same cows in the afternoon. He has walked tobacco fields, assessing the harvest to pay his taxes.

David Mitchell has been a farmer all his life and watched a way of life pass in front of him. At the time of this writing. Mitchell no longer operated a dairy farm, since so few can make it profitable today.

Mitchell and his family have lived on this bucolic land along Mitchell Bend of the Holston River in Grainger County since before modern conveniences arrived here. A large barn to hold hay and other farm equipment was built in 1942. The barn, with its self-supporting roof, stored hay and machinery. Nearby is what David calls a hog oiler, a large round container slick with oil. Hogs rubbed against it to get oiled, which kept down lice infestation.

David Mitchell spent nearly forty-three years milking a cow herd twice a day. Later, he added a herringbone parlor-type operation where he could milk four cows at a time, with four more waiting in line to be milked.

The herringbone milk machine resembles a fishbone. The fish's ribs represent the cows, facing outward, and the fish spine is the milker's area.

Then, he said, his equipment just wore out. He and his family began selling beef cattle, which continues, as of this writing.

David Mitchell recalls growing up on the farm in Grainger County, Tennessee.

Dairy farms, he said, are almost a thing of the past, since it is so labor intensive. It has been difficult to find people who are willing to work that hard anymore. Milking cows is a twice-a-day chore, seven days a week.

David and his wife, Judy, had their dairy farm for right at forty-three years. They have been at it full-time for most of those years, having taken only one vacation during that time when they visited Michigan's Mackinac Island, located to the northeast in the Mackinac Straits. The island itself is a pistachio-shaped island in Lake Huron at the eastern end of the Straits of Mackinac, between the state's Upper and Lower Peninsulas.

David and his family of farmers milked two times a day, 6:00 a.m. and 4:00 p.m., and they also planted corn, soybeans and hay crops.

At one stretch, David worked more than five years consecutively without a day off. Farming, he said, is a way of life. You must work through illnesses and without vacations.

He stopped his dairy farming on May 6, 2012. Today, they purchase 1,000-pound steers and fatten them to 1,500 to 1,600 pounds before butchering and selling the meat to restaurants and some independent meat markets. When this was written, David estimated he sells about 800 pounds of hamburger meat a week to Stock and Barrel restaurant on Market Mall in Knoxville.

David has been feeding cattle all his life. They (his grandfather W.T. Mitchell and father) took their meat to Lays Packing House and East Tennessee Packing Company in Knoxville. He remembered his grandfather and father taking hogs and cattle across the Gay Street Bridge in Knoxville to sell them at East Tennessee Packing Company.

David also recalled seeing a sawmill on the Tennessee River bank adjacent to the East Tennessee Packing Company plant. He said loggers floated logs down river to the mill. Logging operations in Grainger County floated logs down the Holston River to a sawmill in Knoxville.

The Mitchells also sold livestock to Lays. He has a family invoice from 1924 showing that his family sold thirty-four hogs to Lays and received \$858.87 for them (\$0.10 a pound). He also remembered taking Mitchell-harvested tobacco to Dean Planters Warehouse to sell. In 1951, they got

David Mitchell (*center*) is shown with his father, W.T., and son John on their Grainger County farm, where they had a dairy operation for forty years. *Courtesy of David Mitchell.*

$0.31 to $0.36 a pound. In 1924, tobacco brought $0.22 to $0.33 per pound, depending on the grade of the tobacco. Top burley brought $0.60 a pound.

Another outlet in those days for Mitchell produce was the former A&P (Atlantic & Pacific) Stores. The A&P was the first major chain store in the area. Before the big chains arrived, stores were just moms and pops, stands and markets. His family sold produce, fruits and vegetables to those small independent stores and markets.

One of the largest hardware stores at the time was run by the Parker Brothers in Knoxville's Bearden area. In addition to the usual farm implements, Parker also made mule harnesses and were among the first to sell squirrel corn from Mitchell's Farm—squirrel corn being used to feed squirrels in the yards of mostly "city dwellers."

Tobacco, David said, was East Tennessee's main cash crop years back. It was quite labor intensive. At the time, Grainger County was given 1,600 tobacco land allotments by federal regulators when the government began regulating the planting and harvesting of tobacco in the nation.

David Mitchell describes the milking apparatus of his dairy operation in Grainger County. He and his wife and children (John and Becky) operated the dairy for forty years before switching to a beef cattle operation in the 2000s.

The Mitchell farm also raised hogs as part of their farming business. This steel, round looking object, somewhat larger than a basketball, is what is referred to as a "hog oiler." Hogs would rub against the steel ball, and as it rolled around oil would be spread on their skin to help keep insects and other bugs off.

This old, abandoned milk truck was left on the Mitchell farm when the French Broad Dairy business ceased to operate.

Dairy farms have almost disappeared from the landscape of the Appalachian region. Most dairies have sold out to large conglomerate operators or just gone out of business. Pictured here are the remains of the milking apparatus at the Mitchell Farm in Grainger County.

The allotment was based on how much land a farmer owned. The average allotment was about a half acre. Tobacco was such an important crop for East Tennessee farmers from the 1880s up to the start of World War II. In the latter years, tobacco crops paid taxes and sent children to school in new clothes and shoes.

6

CHARLIE CAVIN

Charlie Cavin graduated from the University of Tennessee in 1955 with a degree in agriculture. He became a UT extension agent for Grainger County. After a stint in the military, he spent forty-five years in Grainger County advising farmers and families how to get the most out of the rich soil of the area.

Some farmers credit Cavin with single-handedly turning the Grainger County tomato into one of the best-known farm products in the nation, if not the world.

Cavin, who smiles and laughs easily as he tells one story after the other and in his eighth decade at the time of this interview, grew up in a time and place that is far different than today. He was born in Hawkins County, a rural East Tennessee county that bumps up against the Virginia border.

Farming was and still is a way of life in Hawkins County, especially around McPheeter Bend where Charlie grew up. McPheeter Bend is near Church Hill, the largest town in the county, according to the 2010 U.S. Census.

Cavin learned farming at an early age in McPheeter Bend. He also got a taste of politics. The area was populated largely with Democratic voters. County politics, he said, were controlled by those of a Republican bent.

As a result, Cavin said with a gleeful smile, not much county assistance was afforded to McPheeter Bend. He recounted the story of a steel bridge over the Holston River. The rickety bridge was floored with wood and required restoration periodically. Getting the bridge its needed repairs, Cavin said, was not the easiest task, since county Republicans were not in the habit of helping Democrats, even with road repairs.

Right: Charlie Cavin grew up on McPheeter Bend in Hawkins County but has lived in Grainger County for over fifty years. He was an agricultural extension agent for the University of Tennessee.

Below: Charlie Cavin's father (*center, with white apron*) operated a small country store in Hawkins County during the early twentieth century. He has local produce displayed along with canned goods and general merchandise. *Courtesy of Charlie Cavin.*

Charlie Cavin, who lived in a farm home with his wife, Virginia, when this interview took place, on seven acres they purchased around 1964 for $7,000, acknowledged not too much has changed in Grainger County since the 1800s. Life is still a slow pace, but some of the older ways, and many smaller family farms, have slipped over the edge of time.

His is a typical rural farmhouse in Rutledge, the county seat. The house has tin roof shingles and two rain cisterns but is on the city's water line. When he purchased the house, it didn't have electricity or plumbing.

"I couldn't make a down payment on a free meal back then," he said with a typical Cavinism that has become so popular with the people of the county. And yes, he knows practically everyone in the county, their children and grandchildren.

The house is built so low it does not have a basement or a crawlspace. An ancient farm bell sits atop a pole near the backdoor. "I bought that bell from an old man in the Buffalo community. I saw it lying out in the weeds and

Opposite: Charlie Cavin shows writer Fred Brown an egg basket, a common household item in the early days, now only decoration.

Right: Rocking chairs like this one that Charlie Cavin owns were and are a mainstay of the Appalachian homestead. Enjoyment comes from just rocking and thinking, most times about nothing in particular.

Below: This knife belonged to Carlie Cavin's great-grandfather who fought for the Confederacy during the American Civil War.

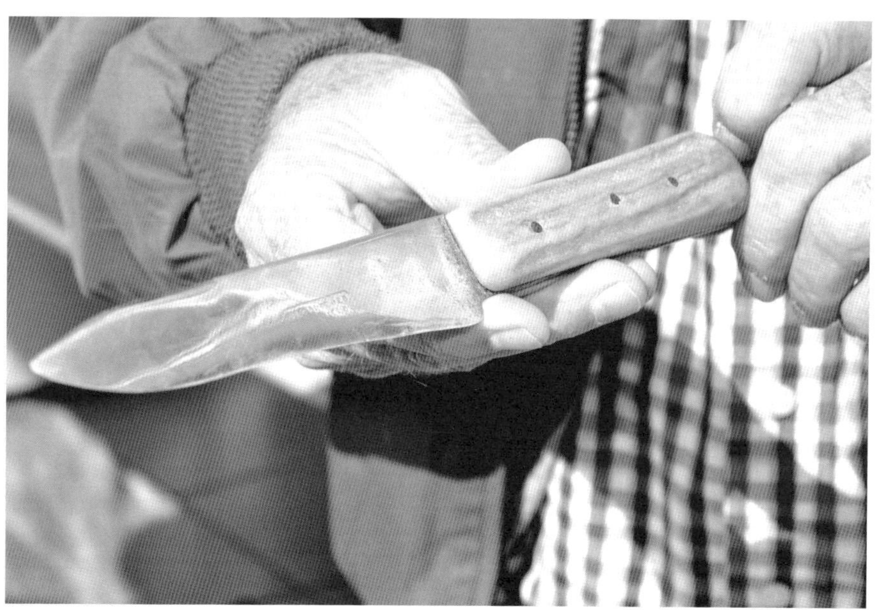

asked Roy Manley, the farmer, about it. 'Give me $10 and put it in the back of your car and keep your mouth shut.'" Which Charlie did.

His house and farm also came with a smokehouse, where he cured hams and pork shoulders at one time. The meat was cured with salt, which Charlie said would eat the nails right out of the floor and walls. Today, the smokehouse serves as a place he keeps his "hand-me-downs"—such as water pumps, scythes, chicken feeders, nail kegs, a sausage mill, milk can, an iron kettle his mother once used for washing, a wood bucket and apple butter stirrer. A rocker sits nearby.

His home is also something of a view back in time. He has the old radio on which he heard the news of the bombing of Pearl Harbor. Other family treasures include a family china cabinet from before the Civil War.

"You live in a home long enough and it becomes home," said Charlie.

Charlie told the story of his great-grandmother who lived through the Civil War. She shared with him stories of people hiding their cattle, chickens and household valuables because soldiers from both sides would steal anything they could, especially food. Desperate soldiers would even kill for food, taking what a farm offered.

His great-grandfather fought with the Twenty-Ninth Tennessee Regiment, Company K, in the Confederacy, a rarity in East Tennessee. Checking to see if a soldier lying on the battlefield was surely dead, he would jab a knife into the heel of the prostrate soldier to make sure he was indeed deceased.

If the soldier moved, then he would shoot him. The knife, which his great-grandfather kept hidden in his boot, was long like a butcher knife. It had a stag handle.

Thinking the knife was special, even though it was old and rusting, Charlie chrome-plated the blade in the 1950s. His great-grandfather was captured by Union soldiers and sent to a prison in Ohio until his release in 1865.

Today, Charlie wishes he had never chromed over the blade. It ruined the value.

Farming has changed dramatically since his youth. But riding over the mountainous and valley-strewn county, land stretches out into lazy layers of color. The land's history is still visible underneath the roll of time. Its farming bones are visible in the lean of fences and the sag of barns, bleached gray from weather and wear. Cows feed on the greensward in leisurely movements.

Where once dirt roads led to plowed furrows, land lies fallow or dotted with large rolls of browning hay. Family gardens are here and there, but not as conspicuous as a half century ago.

Change, Charlie Cavin said, has come to Grainger County, despite the slow seep of time. Tomatoes are royalty in county farming annals. It is fortunate Charlie Cavin figured out years ago how to make the tomato harvest coincide with the seasons.

Instead of honeybees pollinating tomato plants, which brought the tomatoes to harvest when the public buying market was down, Charlie took note of the lowly bumblebee. It, too, is a pollinator.

He told his farmers to purchase bumblebees and turn them loose in hothouses. Grainger County tomato farmers have dotted the landscape with sheer plastic sheets and rolls, hothouses with pollinating bumblebees. The legendary Grainger County tomato was born anew. Today, over seventy different farms raise tomatoes and cultivate about five hundred acres of tomatoes in Grainger County.

Charlie Cavin laughs and rambles on to another story of another time in his county.

7
BILLY LAY

In ways large and small, Billy Lay was shaped by Hogskin Valley in Grainger County, where he was born. He grew up on a 1930s farm in which the day was built around work in confined endeavors—the garden, henhouse, hog pen, barn, smokehouse. Fields were plowed with mules, not tractors. Cows were milked by hand, not machines. Hogs were fed by the buckets of slop and shorts poured into wooden troughs, not metal corn feeders. This was a true Appalachian farm in the hands of a true Appalachian family.

Billy's father, Bert Lay, born in 1905, started the farm on eighty acres. Bert, Billy Lay said, "farmed all his life." In the years before Billy was born, there was not much else available for a family in the rolling countryside of Grainger County. Farms here were not the broad, flat land and fields of Western Tennessee but rather gentle swells in the valleys formed by Clinch Mountain, which bisects the county. Billy Lay grew up in a household akin to the once-popular television show *The Waltons*.

Bert Lay cultivated tobacco, corn, beans and strawberries for truck farming. He would drive his produce about forty miles south to Knoxville to sell them out of the back of his truck.

Billy spent thirty-two years as a welder for the renowned Dempster Dumpster Company of Knoxville. Billy Lay farmed solely until 1955 when he hired on at the Dempster plant. Afterwards, he farmed at first light, completing his chores, and then rode with thirteen others employed at the Dumpster firm in a van from Tater Valley. After returning home from Knoxville, he farmed at night, taking care of his Hereford cattle herd and checking his tobacco plants.

Left: Billy Lay grew up on a farm in Hogskin Valley in Grainger County; he still raises hogs, a garden, hay and fruit trees.

Below: This is the house where Billy Lay's parents lived and farmed in Grainger County. His present house and farm are nearby.

Billy recalled some of the more interesting characters in the Hogskin/Tater Valley communities were "Hog Fish" Floyd Shelton and a fellow in Rutledge known as Pee Wee. When Pee Wee died, Billy said, his real name appeared in the newspaper obituary, and no one knew who it was.

Another interesting fact about the area is an aging and lopsided coffin-maker's shop on the side of the road on Hogskin Valley Road. The name was Vandergrif Casket Shop, owned by Parnick Vandergrif. It is now owned by Larry Lay, Billy's first cousin. The last casket made there was in 1941, Billy said. A vintage glass jar provides a kind of makeshift ceiling light fixture. The jar is screwed in over one of the few lights in the old shop, constructed of slab wood usually found on area barns.

Parnick, Billy said, made caskets out of cherry, pine and cedar wood. He would leave the caskets unfinished until someone ordered one. Then he would put inner lining and place the hardware. Lou Ann Jarvis sewed the casket's inner linings.

Parnick was also something of a character and once climbed to the very top of a tree on Log Mountain. He began acting like a treed fox, Billy said, so several men hunting fox cut the tree down. It almost killed Parnick, Billy recalled with a chuckle.

The old two-room schoolhouse still stands in the Hogskin/Mount Eager community in northern Grainger County. This school is known as Lay School.

A smokehouse was a necessary structure on farms in Appalachia where meat was cured and stored. Bill Lay stands in the door of his smokehouse in Hogskin Valley. He holds a wooden paddle that is used to scrape the floating fat from the boiling water when a hog is butchered on the farm.

Another landmark in the area is Lay School, built in 1913 on an acre donated for the school by Billy's grandfather Charlie. Billy noted the Lays continue to own the school. There was an agreement that if the school ever shut down, the land would revert to the Lay family.

The old school building stands sentinel near Hogskin Valley Road and Lays Gap Road. Constructed of horizontal lathes of sawed weatherboard, the building is crowned with a bell tower and sheltered beneath a silver tin roof. The school remains an empty sign of the past.

In those days, Billy's father and others would "oil" the school floors to keep down dust that was blown inside from the dirt road just above the school.

The one-room school was large enough for about eighty children and one teacher. Each day after school let out, kids would take blackboard erasers across the road and dust them in cedar tree roots. The blackboards remain on the walls today, reminding those who visit the old building of times when chalk instead of computer screens was used for teaching.

Since his family lived near the school, Billy arrived early in the mornings to start a fire in the potbellied stove. He was paid five cents a day for that work. He recalled a couple of teachers who taught at the Lay School. One was Sarah Monroe, a memorable lady who made students do their homework, and Evon Shelton, a strict disciplinarian whom Billy remembers all too well.

The smokehouse, a structure that a farmer used for curing meat with burning wood, usually hickory. Shown in this photo is Billy Lay's smokehouse.

Billy Lay continues to farm, killing hogs when the weather turns colder and curing the hams as he always has in the old smokehouse. But Billy's way of life, simple but wholesome, has all but disappeared.

Asphalted and concreted highways divide farmlands, splitting them asunder. The land becomes part of new estates, creating modern homes that spring up like mushrooms after a fresh rain in fields once planted with crops. Trees are removed not for firewood but to provide acreage that becomes city suburbs.

Gatherings at local grocery stores, where men in baggy overalls and dusty felt hats laughed and talked before buying needed staples that cannot be grown on the farm, are now ghostly thoughts of another time. Once, chickens were bartered for salt. Today, chickens come in frozen packages and salt in small shakers at large chain grocery stores.

Old country stores once supplied farm equipment, nails and tools, along with other necessities for a rural way of life. That page in Appalachia's history has been turned, and a way of life is all but muted by the passage of time.

That wholesomeness that Billy Lay knew has left the land itself.

8

THE CASKET SHOP

The grayed, dried-out building leans along some rocks along Hogskin Valley Road. In the mid-twentieth century, say around the 1930s to the 1940s, the structure served a singular purpose: making caskets for anyone who might need a future box for lasting rest or a family member.

Parnick Vandergrif owned what became known as the casket shop. You had to get your order in early, and you had to leave something of value with Parnick to set up the casket order. Either you or your family picked up the casket when it was needed for the deceased.

The casket shop is in the heart of truck farming land in Grainger County. Land here looks like a farm, green fields stretching beneath long ridges. It was not an easy life, but it was a good life.

At this writing, the old casket shop was owned by Larry Lay, a first cousin to Billy Lay, one of the old families of the Hogskin Valley. Billy remembers that the last casket made in the shop was in 1941.

The caskets were made of cherry, pine and cedar. They were unfinished until they were ordered, then Parnick put in the inner lining and the hardware. Lou Ann Jarvis, who lived nearby, made the linings.

The casket building still stands alongside a gray rock wall made of slabs of limestone pulled from the lands of Hogskin Valley. These rocks lay buried beneath the land surface for millions of years only to find them as part of a casket shop.

The Vandergrif Casket Shop is barely standing, being propped up with a large pole. The proprietors made their last casket in 1941.

Pieces of casket handles remain in the old structure some seventy-five years after the last casket was made there.

Evocative of passing time, a casket handle lies unused and dust covered in the old Vandergrif Casket Shop in Hogskin Valley, Grainger County.

The inside of the Vandergriff Casket Shop shows how much the building has deteriorated since 1941, the year it was last in business.

9

BEN, THE ADVENTURER

The rugged landscape of Appalachia lured the daring explorer and those in search of a new and different life from the environs of the occupied East Coast of North America inland to a land that was later called Appalachia. To discover something new, a place unseen before, and opportunities not realized by others is a unique characteristic of humanity. For thousands of years, people have pushed into uncharted territory to see what lay there, what challenging landscape they might encounter and conquer. Fearless and drawn by the unknown, humans have pushed into the far reaches of not only our planet but even out into the emptiness of space and marveled with awe.

Many of these explorers charted the unusual places of Appalachia. Native Americans who first explored the mountains and ridges and valleys did so, searching for food and living spaces. Later, white Europeans arrived and rediscovered the land and charted its rivers and streams, animal trails and mountainous landscape. Many of these explorers were unknown, and others made history. Some were just people wanting to scratch out a living on this terrain of ridges and valleys, rocky plateaus and forested mountains.

As populations grew and towns and cities were born, some people wanted to be away from the crowded streets and neighborhoods and connect with the wild spaces. One such man was Ben Ballinger, who was fearless and dared to live out his life in a most unusual location, a cave.

Initially, Ben Ballinger said that he wanted to get away from the city life of Knoxville, Tennessee, and contemplate the loss of a girlfriend to another suitor. He had nowhere to go, as times were hard in the 1930s and he was fresh out of the U.S. Navy and unemployed, as many were during that time. His uncle had a farm in a rural part of Jefferson County in the Mill Springs community and told Ben he could come there and scratch out a living if he so chose. A large limestone bluff along the clear waters of the Holston River was located on a farm adjacent to Ben's uncle's farm.

As his story was told to this author, Ben eventually found a cave on that rock bluff and set up housekeeping. His most unusual lifestyle was discovered by local newspapers, and many stories were written about Ben, the cave man. As a result of the media attention, many people were curious about the man who decided to live in a cave. They often visited Ben in the rural Mill Springs community.

Ben was small, with leathery tan skin and a lean build. He discovered he had carpentry skills while building a door to cover the cave entrance and while constructing wooden steps up the bluff to his cave home. Ben eventually gained the trust and friendship of local folks. This resulted in friendships and his building twelve homes in the community.

His life in the cave began in December 1939 and ended in August 1969 when he passed away, a stint of almost thirty years. He cut people's hair, made homebrew drink, built not only houses but also many a boat for local fishermen and told many a story about his life living in a cave. He once told this writer that he lived on no more than $300 a year, an unheard-of feat these days.

The small, musty-smelling cave was about fifty feet long and about eight feet high along the center and wide enough to place a few of his things. The cave formed in limestone layers hundreds of millions of years old, originally in a shallow sea but now part of East Tennessee's landscape.

Ben had a cast-iron wood-burning stove in the cave that he used to cook his meals and to keep fresh brewed coffee day and night. An old army cot was his bed, and a homemade rocker was his chair of choice, which was in front of the stove. A metal smoke pipe vented the stove exhaust to the outside through a wooden façade and door located at the cave entrance.

He became friends with the critters that lived in and around the cave. "The frogs made their yearly jaunt out of the cave to the river last night," he once told me. He laughed as he commented, "They hopped single file, right by my cot and rocker, and right out the door to the outside." He kept an old pistol and shotgun for snakes and bobcats and wild ones of the two-legged kind, he told me.

One time the winter was so severe that ice formed over the rock bluff and slowly covered the cave entrance door and trapped Ben in the cave. A neighbor came by to check on Ben due to the bad weather and found Ben's cave door completely iced over, with Ben still inside the cave. Ben had enough chopped wood inside the cave to keep him warm for a few hours, but he was almost out of firewood when his neighbor came to the rescue and chopped enough of the ice away from the door so Ben could get out and restock his wood supply.

Life for Ben Ballinger was not easy, but it was simple. A sign that hung above his cave door said it all: "Live Better for Less."

10
PAUL RICHARDSON

A trek to the western part of Tennessee shows the similarity of some aspects of our culture in Appalachia to those who live west of Appalachia. Many are descendants of those families that migrated west from Appalachia. Most continued their agrarian craftsmanship but farming large tracts of land not impeded by mountains, rock bluffs, ridges and deep river valleys. This land was rolling to almost flat in topography and very fertile. Agriculture was then and still is today mostly the dominant way of life in western Tennessee. The following accounts are examples of the agricultural lifestyle in the early twentieth century and now in the twenty-first century.

As change invades the lands of Appalachia and dissolves the cultural heritage of its region, adjoining areas of Tennessee are experiencing the change as well. The land of the grand division of West Tennessee is rich in history and culture and has been affected by the change in culture that has taken place over the past one hundred years. As in East Tennessee, dirt roads became gravel roads which later became paved roads. Communities were strong, vibrant, and close-knit. Community people knew one another and would often visit in one another's homes.

Paul Richardson, ninety-three at the time of this interview, was a retired farmer and veteran of World War II who grew up and farmed in the West Tennessee county of Crockett County. He worked behind a pair of plow mules all day breaking up a field. He also logged and used mules for pulling the downed trees out of the Cypress Bottoms area of Crockett County.

Paul Richardson, World War II veteran of Alamo, Tennessee, has seen major changes in our culture during his ninety-four years of living in Tennessee, including the disappearing of our agriculture heritage and loss of community schools.

They lived in a wood frame house. They were renters as opposed to sharecroppers. Renters paid rent but had their own equipment. Sharecroppers did not own anything; the landowner had to furnish everything.

When Paul was a young man, he logged after his family completed the crop season for the year. He would cut timber in the river and creek bottoms. They sold their logs to sawmills, but they had to use mules to drag the logs out of the bottoms and to the sawmills. They cut cypress, poplar and gum, mostly. After the sawmill cut the timber into planks, the mill kept a portion of the sawed lumber as payment for processing the remaining lumber. The families who logged would use the scraps as stove wood to use when cooking or heating homes.

Paul was logging the day he heard about the bombing of Pearl Harbor and knew he would be leaving his community soon for war. Before departing for the war in Europe in 1943, Richardson helped his parents buy a farm in the Crockett County community of Nance. He planned to return home after the war and farm with his father.

He said that the main crops that they farmed during the 1920s and '30s were cotton, oats, hay and corn. When he returned home from the war, he rejoined his father in farming in the Crockett County community of Nance. He said that he hand-chopped weeds from the rows of cotton and picked the cotton by hand.

Farmers had to know their terrain to know where to grow their crops. They also knew how to get out of the weather and stay out of the wind, low areas, tree lines, old, abandoned buildings and so on. Just common-sense things, he said. He began his farm chores when he was seven years old. He would take care of the mules each day, feeding them food like oats and corn in the morning and then hay in the evening.

The biggest change he experienced in farming is the increase in mechanization. His family had four mules and farmed 50 acres in the 1920s and 1930s. Today, one person can farm 1,500 acres alone, using GPS equipment and computers on exceptionally large equipment and

Above: Paul Richardson's father (*on horse*) was still using a horse and buggy when Paul was born in 1921. *Courtesy of the Paul Richardson family.*

Opposite: Paul Richardson used horses to get around on his farm in Crockett County up into the 1960s. Richardson also used mules when he was a teenager to haul logs from the swamp lands, before World War II. *Courtesy of the Paul Richardson family.*

understanding the intricacies of soil science, fertilizers and the mechanization of production.

Rural living in the 1930s and '40s was not easy. Homes did not have conveniences that we take for granted today: water was hauled from a well or cistern; heat was derived from wood, oil or coal stove; light was from oil lamps; homes were rarely insulated; and bathrooms were outhouses. Cooking was done on wood-burning cast-iron stoves and clothes' washing was by hand. Paul said that the kitchen was the warmest place in the house, winter and summer.

In fact, Richardson recalled electricity arrived in his section of Crockett County in the late 1930s. In East Tennessee, the Tennessee Valley Authority, created in 1933, provided electricity for the region, bringing lights to many a darkened household for the first time.

He remembered when TVA contractors started pulling electric lines across fields, from pole to pole. He used his pair of mules to help pull the lines; the mules were especially effective pulling lines across creeks, swamps and soft ground.

TVA paid Paul eight dollars an hour for using the mules and seventy-five cents to one dollar a day for Paul's labor; he would work about ten hours a day. He remembered that when the people first got electricity, they would leave the lights on in their home all day and night, because it was so new and different. They did not know what it was going to cost. When they started getting their electric bill, then they changed their behavior. When electricity replaced the oil and kerosene lamps, home life changed forever.

Most all communities had a school, church and store, which sold all manner of necessities. Things like barbed wire, hand tools, axes, shovels, staple goods, cloth and shoes. But the demise of the rural community school, Richardson noted, began the decay of the rural community. Education was highly valued, and schools were usually located in the center of the community, where children would not have to walk or ride a bicycle more than a few miles to attend. There were no carpools in the 1920s, 1930s and 1940s.

Community stores were commonplace in most rural areas, providing the necessary staples like flour, sugar, meal, bacon and coffee. Many of the old stores were a combination of country store and hardware outlet. Some even bartered for fresh chickens and sold caskets, nails, garden tools and barbed wire. And most stores offered credit throughout the year, relying on being paid after fall harvest season when the farmers would be paid for their bounty.

Richardson remembered that cars began to make a larger appearance in the rural areas in the late 1930s. Although many families owned a Model T or Model A, people mostly walked or rode a horse or horse and buggy for transportation. He said that the windshields on the cars would keep wind and bugs and other things off people's faces. He remembered that transportation began with the horse and buggy and gradually changed to cars in the 1920s and 1930s and became mostly cars and trucks in the late 1930s.

He also remembered that most roads were dirt up until just before World War II. Some major roads were paved with tar and gravel and later some form of asphalt. Country roads were either dirt or gravel with oil sprayed over the gravel, to keep down dust. The dirt roads were very muddy during wet weather periods and full of big potholes. They were not the kind of roads you could make time on like today's roads.

Richardson remembered coming home from World War II. Ironically, it was December 7 (same date as the Pearl Harbor attack, but four years later) when he arrived in Jackson, Tennessee, late at night, after midnight. When he got off the bus, he looked around for a taxi. He found a taxi nearby, and the driver said he would take Paul home for free since he was a veteran coming home from war. He drove Paul to Alamo and then on out to the rural Nance Community. When they got to his road, he told the driver to stop and he would walk the rest of the way. The road was dirt and muddy with deep potholes and Paul was afraid the taxi would get stuck and wake everybody up; it was about 2:00 a.m. So, the taxi driver let Paul out and he walked the last half mile to his home. He was met about halfway there by his three-legged dog, Bo Diddle. They walked to his house, where his sisters and parents met them.

Richardson said, "When you lose control of what you do locally, then it is a bad thing." Some examples of those choices, he said, include how to educate your children, how to live your life and, now, which doctors to use. "People used to know their neighbors, they would help each other out in hard times; everybody knew all the families in the community; today, very few people know their neighbors," Richardson said.

11

DANIEL JACOBS

Farming in Appalachia continues to change as new and innovative agricultural techniques are developed and employed. Although not located in Appalachia per se, West Tennessee is considered the leader in Tennessee for row crop production and compares well to the farming culture of Appalachia. The family farm has all but vanished, replaced by mega farms and corporate agribusiness conglomerates. However, a few small-sized farm businesses continue to flourish as young and energized well-educated farmers have taken up the responsibility of feeding the masses.

Daniel Jacobs is one such young farmer. Jacobs was raised in Hardeman County in West Tennessee. He first lived in Bolivar and then moved to Hickory Valley, Tennessee, when his parents, Lynda and Danny Jacobs, bought a farm and expanded their business. He grew up on a farm and experienced what farming was about as his parents successfully farmed over two thousand acres of row crops during the mid to late 1990s.

After Jacobs graduated from the University of Tennessee at Martin, he decided that he was going to continue the lifestyle of farming that his parents introduced to him. At age thirty-eight, Jacobs now farms approximately three thousand acres of row crops in Hardeman County and raises cotton, soybeans and corn. He, his wife, Lacy, and three children are one of an exceedingly small number of young families adopting the farming lifestyle.

One big difference in Jacobs's approach to farming as compared to his parents and grandparents is that he is using what is termed as "precision agriculture." This is where farmers learn the technique of "repeatability of

One of the younger Tennessee farmers is Daniel Jacobs, who farms almost three thousand acres in West Tennessee. Computer programs and input data integrated with his tractor equipment allow him to better and more efficiently farm his land. The non-use of farm livestock to till and plant crops is a major change in our culture from the use of livestock-drawn farm equipment.

cost savings" while growing crops. He learned how to take soil samples on a programmed grid, usually five acres, which is referenced to a GPS unit. The soil tests are performed, and the results are placed into a computer spreadsheet where they are then integrated into the farming equipment onboard computers for application out in the field.

By using the GPS-oriented soil test results, the tractor can spread the exact amount of fertilizer over a field that was previously sampled, changing the application rate as the tractor moves across the field. This procedure applies the precise mixture of fertilizer needed for the soil in each location in the field. This saves fertilizer costs and increases production rates.

The soil tests performed include the pH level, CEC levels (cation exchange captivity—the ability for the plant to absorb or capture the added fertilizer portions), nitrogen, phosphorus, potassium and boron. The precise place the sample is taken is recorded with the GPS unit so it can be applied later in the fertilization process.

Jacobs said that in the few years that he has been farming, the technology has improved tremendously. Today, he plugs in the computer to his tractor and the equipment attached to his tractor and then fertilizes a field with the computer actually driving the tractor. If he chooses to, he can just sit behind the steering wheel and watch as the tractor moves across a field applying the exact amount of fertilizer needed for the crop he is planting. He said that this process is also used in planting the crop seed and in spraying the crop for weeds, insects and disease.

Jacobs reflects on the new technology being incorporated into agriculture. He has a guidance screen now for his tractor that will show him in the field what he has covered with his fertilizing or planting, so if he goes over the

Above: This shows the instrument panel in one of Daniel Jacobs's tractors. His tractor cab also has a stereo radio, air conditioning and computer hookups. A computer screen is shown in upper right.

Left: This computer screen in Daniel Jacobs's tractor is GIS and GPS connected. His tractor, shown in center of screen, is being tracked by satellite. The field he is working on is represented by color and grid lines on the computer screen.

same place, the equipment will not spray or plant in that place he has already covered because it knows where it has been due to the GPS unit. Jacobs said, "This saves money."

Now compare this modern process with that of his parents or grandparents to understand the "leap" that technology has given to the practice of farming. Gone are the teams of mules that his grandfather would use to plow fields or the numerous field hands needed to till the ground, plant and harvest the crop.

Jacobs has studied his farming operation and understands what he can produce for a cost per acre. As an example, in 2013 he produced 1,016 pounds of cotton per acre of ground; 40 bushels of soybeans per acre; 135 bushels of corn per acre; and 80 bushels of wheat per acre.

This photo shows a portion of a twenty-four-row planter that Jacobs uses to plant his crops. Farm equipment has become hi-tech in today's computerized world.

To better understand how much Jacobs produces, the discussion can be equated to a common product; take corn for example. Everyone knows what an ear of corn is and how many ears of corn a person can eat. Jacobs plants about 28,000 to 29,000 seeds (plants) of corn per acre, of which about 25,000 to 26,000 plants survive. Equating one ear of corn per plant, that equals about 25,000 ears of corn per acre that he produces. If he raises 100 acres of corn, that equals about 2.5 million ears of corn. Now, how many people can he feed with that amount of corn? Oh, and by the way, a single stalk (plant) of corn can produce several ears of corn.

Today, about 1 percent of the population of Tennessee is involved in agriculture, according to the Tennessee Farm Bureau organization. Fewer and fewer people are engaged in farming, especially in Appalachia. Jacobs sees a few more young people getting into farming, but not many. "The work is too hard for most. Most cannot just jump into farming because of the costs involved. Most people that do farm inherited a family farm or use their parents' equipment and fields. Most are family farms. Most of my friends tend to live on family-owned land," Jacobs said.

Most of the farmers Jacobs knows have families who also work the farm. The farmers in the rural community of Hardeman County where he farms tend to lend a helping hand when one of them needs help (weather disaster or death in the family). They also tend to be patriotic, honest and hardworking. "They do what they say they will do," he commented. "There are always a few bad apples, but the vast majority are very good people." This attitude is pervasive in the Appalachian region today, where farms are generally small but worked well.

Jacobs thinks that family farms are vanishing due to the hard work, costs and uncontrollable factors. The main competition to family farms is the big corporate farmers, the big business–type farms. "They seem to try to run the small farmer out of business by out bidding for rental land or buying farms. The family farms also tend to have the land leased in their respective communities, which tends to limit new farmers from getting enough land to farm."

Jacobs concluded, "Farming is a way of life, not just a job; you have to love it, or you would not do it." He continued by saying that farmers really have little control on the variables of farming, like weather, market factors, input costs, fuel prices that change daily, disease, equipment breakdowns and more. "It is a big gamble." You need to have crop insurance to balance out the uncontrollable factors.

So it goes in the land of West Tennessee and Appalachia as well. Small family farms dot the landscape, but not as many today as in years past. Those that do choose to farm do so as "part-time" farmers, holding a second job elsewhere and working the farm after returning home from the day job. A few are still farming the family farm, but costs, hard work and not enough land keep the number of farmers low.

PART III

OLD STRUCTURES AND SUNDRIES

12
APPALACHIA INFRASTRUCTURE

I recall exploring an old, abandoned mill in my younger days. It was a brick structure historians say was built around 1800. The windows were mostly broken, and the doors nailed shut. My cousin and I strolled up to the mill house and dared each other to go in. The outside steps to the side door we could see had rotted into a pile of soft brown decayed wood.

We found some stones from a nearby limestone outcrop and piled them up to the entrance. Pushing gently on the weathered gray wooden door, we saw blackness beyond the opening and wanted to go exploring.

Thin rays of bluish-gray light sliced through the emptiness of the main room of the mill. We could faintly see wooden beams with sections of rope hanging down, piles of burlap bags mixed with paper sacks that were used for bagging the milled grain. Spiderwebs drifted in the air along with the dust of ground-up corn and wheat left from past days of milling.

Step by step we inched farther into the darkness, wooden boards squeaking and popping beneath our shoes. We saw the finely honed wooden chutes hanging down from where the grain flowed when first brought in by the local farmers and "dumped" into the holding vats. Chains and leather belts were strung among the rafters and beams, being held up from the floor level and kept from tangling with other equipment.

Noticeable was the state of change the equipment and building had undergone due to non-use and neglect. As the culture changed from local gristmills to large milling factories, so did the structures and community buildings change that were left behind. Wood rotting, roofs decaying; communities left for towns and cities; attitudes and cohesiveness for larger cities and diversity.

Throughout the lands of Appalachia, the infrastructure exhibits its own distinctive way in that it is part of the culture. Most roads began as animal paths that were used by the settlers and became dirt roads when horses, mules and oxen were the chosen mode of travel. The way the roads are constructed is often dictated by the rugged topography; curvy roads are necessary to traverse over ridges and mountains. River crossings were often made by ferries that were propelled by farm animals and the river currents; in some instances, water crossings were bridged with wooden structures and replaced with overhead steel-truss construction that is today being replaced with steel-reinforced concrete structures.

Many communities began at crossroads. Blaine Crossroads, Halls Crossroads, to name a couple that still exist today. The early roads were once dirt (mud when it rained), then transitioned to gravel, which were most common. Other crossroads became towns and cities that have mostly continued to flourish today.

Remnants of past farm home sites are marked with rusting farm equipment, car bodies and weathered and decaying lumber from houses and farm structures.

Many tales have been shared on the front porches of country stores like this one at the Grainger-Union County line just outside of Maynardville, Tennessee.

Some of the more common structures of old include the country store, churches and one- and two-room schoolhouses. The old country store where one could buy or barter for flour, eggs, tobacco, farm tools, barbed wire, a gun or axe and clothing was once a popular fixture in most Appalachian communities. High-steepled church buildings, usually painted white and of wood construction, were also fixtures of rural communities. Along with the stores and churches were the schoolhouses that each community tended to have and operate—often with several grades grouped together in one room, some with all twelve grades together.

East Tennessee is blessed with wonderful settlement history. The Appalachian region of East Tennessee was a gateway to the rest of the state in the eighteenth century. It developed quicker than other parts of the state and established not only laws but also buildings to conduct the county's and state's business. Some of these buildings still abound and are historic structures. Brick was often used to build some of the buildings. That brick was, in many cases, produced right from the land on which the building was to be erected.

Other buildings that characterize Appalachian life include gristmills, barns and houses. Most small communities had a gristmill, where locals would

Many wood structures have decayed and crumbled back into the ground and disappeared like this small, abandoned home in Grainger County.

bring their grain to have ground into flour or meal. The weather-beaten gray barns that dot the landscape have become iconic to the Appalachian region. Different styles of construction can be seen throughout the landscape. In addition, the houses that marked homesteads have mostly disappeared. Log houses and I-houses were most common. Variations of these have lasted on into the mid-twentieth century.

The following accounts have been drawn from interviews with those willing to share their story about life in Appalachia. Some aspects are told with photographs.

13
OLD COUNTRY STORES

One of the most historic features of East Tennessee is the plethora of country or rural stores. Many of those operations, all family owned then, would serve a community from birth till death—meaning the store provided for its community from cradle to grave. Some of the old stores provided cradles for babies and caskets for the deceased. If you were not

This was once a thriving farm store but has since closed its doors; the building is falling into disrepair. Many memories have been made in stores like this one, now vanishing from our landscape.

General stores were once commonplace along rural roads in Appalachia. Today, they are all but gone as the larger food chains and box stores have replaced them. A few of the former buildings remain, like this one near the Grainger-Union County line.

Most earlier stores in Appalachia were built facing the adjacent roadway with the store name painted on the side of the building. One such relic is the Dixon Grocery building in the Sunrise Community along Highway 11-W in Grainger County. The grocery closed in the mid-1950s.

This old, abandoned community store near the Sevier-Cocke County line has seen its last days and will soon be but a forgotten memory. These stores were once community meeting places where people got their staples, exchanged messages and got their news.

Seemingly lost to memories, old community stores such as this one near the Jones Cove section of Cocke County gradually disappear as neglect and deterioration take over these forgotten structures.

Coca-Cola
Tuckahoe
Trading Post
Coca-Cola
MILK
8908
ICE
ICE

BIC lighter
Coca-Cola
MATADOR
MATADOR
ENQUIRER

Opposite, top: Neighborhood grocery stores are a thing of the past, such as Tuckahoe Trading Post located in a rural section of east Knox County. The store building was destroyed by fire in 2015, a couple of weeks after this photo was taken.

Opposite, bottom: In the past, grocery stores used to keep a credit ledger on each customer who bought goods on credit. This cash register and credit ledger was last used in the old Foust Grocery Store that was once in the Grainger County community of Blaine. Each customer had a tab; it listed the goods that were purchased and the dollar value charged. This photo was made at the Blaine IGA Grocery Store, now closed.

This page, top left: Signs placed on the side of buildings, such as stores and gas stations, were once commonplace. Many such signs advertised soft drinks like Coke and RC Cola. These old signs are fast disappearing from the landscape along with some of the products they advertised.

This page, top right: Old advertising signs were once common sightings on the front and sides of old stores, like this old Coke sign.

This page, bottom: Old general stores have all but disappeared in the Appalachia region. A few remain like the Cumberland Mountain General Store in Clarkrange, Tennessee. A good meal can be had at this store. Diners can also stock up on antiques of choice.

This weather-beaten store building tells of times past when common purchase items were advertised on the storefronts. This abandoned structure was found in the mountainous area of Unicoi County, near Flag Pond, Tennessee.

Gas stations used to be common as part of the operation of community general stores. Most are now gone and replaced by the quick mart type of gas station and store. Shown here is the old gas pump and store in Valle Crucis, North Carolina, near the larger mountain town of Boone, just over the Tennessee–North Carolina state line.

birthing or dying, the store also sold hardware for farmers, traded with those same farmers for fresh eggs, chickens and vegetables. They also brought in some of the latest in materials for dresses and other pretty frills for farm wives. Hard candy for children was a given, as was tobacco. The country store in a way was the center of many communities. In many instances, the store also housed the post office, bringing in people to gather and to talk. In many cases, during political elections, the store served as a center for voting and counting votes. Its disappearance has brought about a distinct change in rural East Tennessee—the community store is now a rarity that has allure for tourists.

14

THE OLD STORE

There are not many like the old country store at the corner of Piedmont and McGuire Roads in Jefferson County, Tennessee. Jan Reagan owns and runs the store built by Bill Brooks in 1901. H.F. Snodderly purchased the store in 1940 and ran it for three years before heading off to World War II. When he returned, Snodderly repurchased the place and operated it until 1987.

In the 1990s, Jan Reagan learned that if she did not buy the store, the current owner planned to tear it down. That, she said, could not happen.

The Crossroads, the store's location, was once known as Mount Crossroads. The store and the crossroads are in the shadow of the Piedmont Mountains, just north of Highway 25W.

At one time in the store's history, the proprietor traded fresh chickens for groceries. Fresh eggs were also traded. When this was written, a portion of the store continued to stock some of the old-time farm equipment, like nuts and bolts, plumbing supplies and grocery items. But today the store is mainly a gathering place for those living in the area or those who know where to find home cooking.

Jan and her "women" open the store at seven o'clock every morning, specializing in homemade biscuits and sausage. Bacon, ham tenderloin, gravy and biscuits, sausage eggs and biscuits are also on the menu. At noon, the menu switches to hamburgers, cheese sandwiches, ham, bologna, corn beef, chicken and dumplings, fried okra, coleslaw, cornbread and tea, all for a low, low $6.29 (at the time of this interview).

Above: Few general stores remain in the Appalachian region. This one, known as the Piedmont General Store, began its history in 1901 and is in the Piedmont community of Jefferson County. Work boots, nails and screws and a sandwich are a few of the items that can be had in this establishment.

Right: Old-time cooking can be found at the Piedmont General Store in Jefferson County. Owner Jan Regan serves an apple stack cake to patrons at the store, one of just a handful of general stores left in operation in East Tennessee.

And if you visit, be sure to try the store's stack cake. It is unmatched.

Country stores are disappearing practically overnight, unable to compete against the huge chain box stores, the strip mall outlets and the Internet. This means something dear is leaving the landscape, and not just the history.

It is the vanishing of a way of life, a time when people in a community came to their one store where they could get not only groceries, or trade for them, but also talk to their neighbors to catch up on one another. Some old stores also doubled as a post office.

The Piedmont General Store in the Piedmont community of Jefferson County is one of the very few old mom-and-pop community stores remaining in the East Tennessee region. The store began operation in 1901 and has been serving the community continuously since then.

This photograph shows some of the items that used to be sold at the Piedmont General Store. Most of the products and companies illustrated on the products have gone out of business today.

Modern grocery stores just do not have the character of a wood-sided store where the floors were once oiled and still squeak a bit.

And when is the last time you looked up before opening the store's screen door to see a plastic bag filled with water? That is to keep flies out in the summer. Flies, see, will come to the water, and not zoom into the store's open screen that double slaps as a customer ambles inside.

That is character, and it is only found in some of the rarest of places, like Appalachia's country stores, an endangered species. Other country stores are all but gone, except for their decaying structures and the memories that were made there. Those with the memories are slowly passing on, taking with them encyclopedias of information about a time forgotten in our culture.

15

JOE SHEDDAN/MT. HOREB GENERAL STORE

Charlie Gass grew up on Mt. Horeb Road and frequented the Joe Sheddan/Mt. Horeb General Store during the late 1940s to 1960. His grandparents were members of the nearby Lebanon Cumberland Presbyterian Church (established in 1874) and are buried at the adjacent cemetery.

When Charlie Gass was growing up in the Mt. Horeb community of Jefferson County, he said that Joe Sheddan was the owner of the store and ran it himself. Joe had an ancient GMC panel truck that he used to deliver goods to people in the community. The truck had only one seat, so the boys who helped deliver goods had to sit on rickety Coke crates and baskets when they rode in the truck. They mostly delivered feed and seed to area farmers.

Joe Sheddan had a brother who ran a store over on Davis Hollow Road off Highway 92. He had an auto mechanic there and did repairs for locals.

The store is a two-story brick building with a high front facing. There was an old wooden floor with a counter on the left and shelves on the right as you entered the store. The cash register was midway down the counter on the left where all the tobacco products were kept. There was an old potbellied stove in the rear of the store where locals would sit and exchange information (gossip) during the cold months. During warmer months, they (locals) would sit on the front porch of the store to do their information swapping. They mostly talked about community happenings and politics. They would regularly play penny poker as they discussed topics.

Mount Horeb Store in Jefferson County is vine covered and abandoned but still brings good memories to the locals who grew up there buying groceries and sundries and spending time in the store spinning tales.

One of the locals who frequented the store to talk was George Blackburn. He was a man who lived in the area and who engineered the building of an unusual tractor. He connected two tractors together and used them to build area barns. He measured and numbered every board and cut all the boards prior to building each barn.

Inside the store, several of the locals took a silver dollar and screwed it down on the wood floor. Then, they would watch customers try to pick the silver dollar up. Sometimes the customer would put their foot over it and then ease down to pick at their shoe then try to get the dollar coin. They would all laugh and poke fun at the confused customers.

Joe Sheddan sold tobacco products at the store. One of the favorites was chewing tobacco. The chewing tobacco came in long "rope-like" strands. A person could buy five cents' worth or ten cents' worth. He simply measured out the amount the five cents would buy and then cut it off for the customer.

The store also had a meat counter and sold meat products to customers. Charlie, as did the other locals, most enjoyed getting a slice of bologna and a slice of cheese and eating it with crackers at the store. The crackers were the kind of crackers that came in a sheet which you could break into four individual crackers. Today, all the saltines are just one cracker in a stack of crackers. They would quench their thirst with a "dope," what today we call a soda or coke, because Coke contained cocaine until 1929.

The store also sold canned goods, and during the season it offered fresh vegetables, locally grown. It also sold feed and grain and seed. There were some farm materials there like flowerpots and harnesses for livestock. The building is a two-story structure, and upstairs offered clothing for men and women for sale.

Behind the store, Joe Sheddan had two acres of land, and he grew tobacco and a garden there. He raised the tobacco to sell in the store. Charlie Gass remembered that they got electricity on Mt. Horeb Road in 1943. The electricity changed things in the community and the store. Now they had lights.

Gass recalled that four of the local bunch (Sheddan, Tom Bettis, Bill Fox and Charlie Gass) that hung out at the store drove an old GMC panel truck to Cades Cove to camp. While there in Cades Cove, they drove to the old mill area and came upon a family reunion. They just acted like they were part of the family gathering and went through the food line and ate like kings. They even had a dessert table, and they ate there too. No one ever questioned them.

An incident at the store involved two of the locals: George Lyle and Lenis Free. Free was a Republican and proud of it. Lyle called him a Democrat one day and Lenis chased him for a mile with a knife saying, "No one calls me a Democrat!"

The store sold Esso gas (now Exxon-Mobile) and had a pump out front. At first, the pump had a glass ball on top and you would hand pump the gas up into the glass ball, then you would just take the spout attached to the glass ball and put it in the gas tank and let the gas flow free down the hose into your tank. Then they got a pump that had a crank handle and dials that showed you how much gas you had bought along with the price. You had to turn the crank on the side of the pump to reset the dials every time you bought gas. That pump is still there. Charlie said that most people would buy a dollar's worth of gas. Gas cost from eight cents to a dime a gallon.

Charlie said that when he was a boy, there were only four cars in the community. His father was a deputy sheriff there in Jefferson County, and he remembered that his father raided some moonshine stills over on Grapevine Hollow Road near Chestnut Hill. When they raided the moonshiner's place, he got shot in the foot. Another man was shot to death during the raid.

Above: Old gas pumps required one to turn a crank handle to reset the dials on the pump before pumping the gas. Shown here is one such crank handle on the side of an old Esso gas pump located in the Mount Horeb community of Jefferson County.

Left: Old general stores have all but disappeared across the landscape of Appalachia. Pictured here is the Mount Horeb Store, also known as the Joe Sheddan Store. It has been in disrepair for nearly half a century and is quickly being overtaken by vines and weeds.

Charlie is the youngest of nine children. He told this writer that five are still alive. The oldest one alive is ninety-three as of this writing. One is ninety-one, one is eighty-nine, then eighty-seven and Charlie is seventy-seven.

Tom Myers currently owns the store as of this writing. He lives nearby.

16

MARGARET BURKEY, DULANEY GENERAL STORE

When Margaret Burkey stepped off the train in Greeneville, Tennessee, from her home in Massachusetts, she had little notion she would meet her husband that night at the train station. But standing there in the clanking and noise was Dewey Oliver Burkey Jr. along with others to welcome the new Presbyterian missionary to Greene County. She noticed Dewey's friendliness right away.

The Dulaney General Store building still stands in the community where it began operation in 1892. The Dulaney community is in Greene County, Tennessee.

Dulaney General Store, constructed in 1892, stands in the Dulaney community of Greene County, Tennessee.

Margaret Burkey, last owner of the Dulaney General Store, discusses the history of the old store operation.

The year was 1952, and the county was still lush with farmlands, planted fields, dairy farms, row crops and solid farm families. Just for a moment, however, Margaret was a young woman in a strange land. The world was indeed big, and it seemed it had swallowed her.

But Greene County, known for its farms and scenic land views, was nothing if not welcoming and warm to the new missionary. She quickly found her place and noted that Dewey Oliver Burkey was exactly right and fell in love. Dewey was the son of one of three brothers of a distinguished Virginia family who moved to Tennessee in the late 1800s.

Tom Burkey, one of the original three Virginia brothers, built the store and a house in the nearby community of Dulaney near Greeneville. The store was in the back of the house Tom had built. Tom Burkey was father of Dewey Oliver Burkey, who is the last Burkey to own and operate the store.

The store was named the Dulaney General Store and was established in 1892. The store remained in operation until 1955.

17
CHURCHES

As vast as East Tennessee is, with its ridges, valleys and rivers, the region is just as diverse in its religious structures. Some churches found by the authors date to the eighteenth century and many from the nineteenth and twentieth. Many of the wooden structures with bell towers look as if they stepped right out of a picture book.

Dupont Baptist Church in Sevier County is nestled in the foothills along the base of Chilhowee Mountain in the Dupont Springs community.

Community churches are a mainstay of the Appalachian region and dot the rural landscape as well as towns and cities. Many have been restored or well cared for, such as Lebanon Cumberland Presbyterian Church in Jefferson County. The church was established in 1874 in the Mount Horeb community.

Puncheon Camp Baptist Church, Grainger County.

Built around 1901, the Rutledge Presbyterian Church is located on a rise above U.S. Highway 11-W in Rutledge, Tennessee.

Old cemeteries are commonly found in the Appalachian region. These old burial grounds have been well taken care of over the years, and the graves date back well into the nineteenth century. This cemetery contains graves that date to the early 1800s. Primitive Baptist Church in Cades Cove, Great Smoky Mountains National Park.

This church building in the Warrensburg community of Greene County is one of the older congregations in the East Tennessee area. This group organized in September 1793. Many of the older churches in Appalachia have been saved and restored and maintained by the local communities.

Old cemeteries dot the landscape in the Appalachian region, like Sugarlands Cemetery in the Great Smoky Mountains.

Families and church congregations have successfully preserved many of these old spiritual houses, most of which are still in use today. These rural congregations are generally small in number of people and made up of several groups of families. The echo of their voices singing praises to their maker can oft be heard along rural roads on Sunday mornings.

18
SCHOOLHOUSES

Perhaps one of the saddest of stories is how the one-room school just simply vanished from the landscape. No thought of preservation or historic significance. Very few remain, but the authors found some. It is a tribute to the people of their communities who salvaged what was left of a once glorious period in rural education, the one-room school where a dedicated teacher controlled the education of the children of a region.

Most notable about the old schools is the belfry that rests atop the front roof section of the building. These bells were once a community fixture, letting the children and parents know that the school day was about to begin.

The decaying structure of an old school building in rural Appalachia is shown here. Most of these unique structures are gone from the landscape.

Riverdale School still stands as of this writing. Its location in rural east Knox County has kept it out of the mainstream development areas. Non-use and neglect will eventually lead to the decay and collapse of this historic building in Appalachia.

This old school building has the characteristic structure of one room, white weatherboard siding and a bell tower. It is in northern Grainger County, Tennessee.

Island View School in Boyds Creek sits vacant and slowly decaying in a pasture along Boyds Creek Highway in Sevier County.

This two-room schoolhouse characterizes the school days back in the first half of the twentieth century. Lay School, as it is called by the community, still stands in the location it was used, near Log Mountain and Hogskin Creek in Grainger County, Tennessee.

Few of these old structures can be found today, seen mostly in the rural communities of Appalachia, old communities such as Mount Eager, Boyd's Creek, Dotson and Riverdale to name just a few.

PART IV

GRAVEL ROADS, BRIDGES, RIVER FERRY CROSSINGS AND OLD CARS

19
GRAVEL ROADS

I enjoy walking down gravel roads. They are so serene and uncomplicated. Gravel is the main ingredient of the road, while some soil and grass can often be seen woven within the fabric. The limestone gravel, light gray in color, is crushed out of larger slabs and chunks of gray limestone that was formed in shallow seas millions of years ago. As time maneuvered its way through history, so did the limestone change from being in a shallow sea to becoming part of ridges and mountains far away and hundreds of feet above any sea or ocean.

These gravel country roads wind around hills, farmhouses, trees and an occasional gully or rock bluff as they cross the rural terrain. They are so much the fabric of our heritage, a fabric that is soon to disappear from the Appalachian landscape.

Wildflowers flourish along the road borders, where butterflies and other insects nose around the flower heads to gain nourishment and pass along pollen. These clumps of flowers are like bouquets, and the florescence of their bloom brightens the adjoining pastures.

Fences usually border the gravel roads. Some are barbed-wire, others are wood-plank and still others are electric with a single wire strung from post to post. My favorite is the wood rail fence; some are split rail in a cross-wag fashion, while others are just straight-line wood rail fences. Both weather to a gray wood texture that brings heritage back to the area and character to the gravel road.

An occasional car or truck passes by and creates a small dust storm, sending a cloud of gray-white dust out over the adjoining lands. During the drier periods, the dust cloaks the vegetation with gray-white powder, muting their beauty. Walking along a gravel road when a car passes by can send you coughing and rubbing your eyes and thinking, "I wish it would rain a bit to help settle this dust!"

The Appalachian landscape used to be marked by these gravel roads, connecting small communities and farms with each other. Most people just plodded along at slower speeds because the gravel was loose, and vehicles could slide around on the gravel if they moved too fast. The gravel roads would be marked with potholes where mud puddles or just deep depressions in the roadbed formed from the traffic of trucks and cars passing over the softer places in the roadbed. Driving fast over these obstacles risked scraping the bottom of the vehicle or even losing control of it completely.

Over the past fifty to sixty years, many of these old gravel roads have been replaced with paved roads and sometimes with superhighways. They were first oiled to help keep the dust down. Eventually, tar mixed with liquid asphalt was used as a base as it was sprayed over the gravel, then covered with small gravel chips. This method and road type is referred to

Hyatt Lane in Cades Cove is an example of a well-used gravel road in the Great Smoky Mountains National Park.

as a macadam road pavement, which became extremely popular during the forties and fifties.

Earliest roads in Tennessee consisted mainly of dirt paths, Native American trails and animal tracks. Over the years, these early pathways became well-traveled routes by the settlers entering the region of what became Tennessee. This first happened in East Tennessee and then spread westward through Middle and finally West Tennessee.

One of the earliest roads in the Appalachian region was the Great War Path, which coursed its way through Cumberland Gap along the Tennessee and Kentucky state line. It was given its name in 1750 by Dr. Thomas Walker and was later used by Daniel Boone and became known as the Wilderness Road.

In Tennessee, as in the rest of the United States, the period of Reconstruction was not a time of progress in road building. A notable exception was the construction of the first public road system in Tennessee in 1889. By 1900, the automobile craze had hit the United States, where over four thousand autos had been registered, including a whopping forty in Tennessee.

By 1923, over 173,366 vehicles had been registered in Tennessee, and by 1955 the number had risen to 1,104,650 according to the Tennessee State Highway Department records. In 1956, Congress established the Highway Act of 1956, which set up a 41,000-mile system of superhighways called the Interstate and Defense Highway System. Tennessee was allocated an original 1,047.6 miles of interstate mileage, to be completed by 1972. The first section of interstate in Tennessee was a 1.8-mile stretch of Interstate 65 in Giles County that was completed on December 17, 1958.

Today, most public roads are paved, usually with asphalt. These black ribbons of transportation now texture the hills and valleys of Appalachia, making travel much easier, more comfortable and safer. The few gravel roads that are left in the region are usually found in the national parks and forests. This would include the Great Smoky Mountains National Park, Big South Fork of the Cumberland River National Recreation Area and the Cherokee National Forest. Some state, city and county parks still have gravel roads. However, most county system roads are now paved, with a few exceptions.

I remember the many times that I visited my relatives in Jefferson County, Tennessee, where the county roads were gravel. The small Jefferson County community of Mill Springs still had gravel roads up until the late 1950s and early 1960s when I would visit my grandparents who lived there. During the summer months, you could tell if someone drove by on the gravel road by the boil of gray-white dust made by the passing vehicle. You could not drive fast because of the loose gravel; it was like driving on marbles if you drove fast.

Those days are pretty much gone now; replaced with asphalt and concrete. Most would think that the asphalt roads were an improvement, and probably they are correct. However, I do miss the serene winding gravel road that made a sound when a car passed by, or that old farmhouse with the crooked-sitting mailbox that had RFD painted on the side. I reminisce of the days when I would walk down a country gravel road and pick up a handful of gravel and just throw the rocks at a fence post or tree alongside the road. I enjoyed hearing myself walk on the surface, marking my progress as I continued my journey. Yes, those were the days, and they are disappearing.

20

OLD BRIDGES

Roads of the past usually had an old bridge that one had to cross on the way to visit a friend, go to church, buy groceries or even go to work. Of course, we must have the bridges to cross creeks, rivers, gullies or even other roads. However, those timeworn highway bridges are the ones that have character and personality.

Some of the early bridges were short, maybe twenty feet in length. Others were longer, some several hundred feet. The most common bridge type in years past was the old-fashioned wooden bridge, constructed of large timbers that were bolted together and formed simple but functional structures to take you across an anomalous feature, like a stream. All one needed was to get to the other side of the creek. A humble wooden bridge sufficed.

Some wooden bridges had side rails of logs or planks. Others were without side rails, making the crossing somewhat precarious, as you could see over the side and watch the land open up along the bridge route. Most had wooden planks that the vehicle would have to drive on to cross the bridge. These planks would often be loose and vibrate, pop or seemingly groan when the car would go across the bridge. Yes, those were the fun days.

As engineering practice developed new techniques, the truss bridge concept began to take shape. These are the type of bridges that had an exposed frame that was built above the bridge but was integral to the support and stability of the structure. Most of these were built of steel and referred to as steel-truss bridges. These were once commonly found in Appalachia, both in the cities and out in the rural areas as well. They were strong, safe

This old steel-truss bridge, located in the Black Fox Community of Grainger County, represents one of the few remaining such bridges left in rural Tennessee. These old structures are fast being lost as they are replaced with new concrete bridges as we continue to improve our infrastructure.

Left: Steel-truss bridges were once common structures crossing streams and rivers; shown is the German Creek Bridge where State Route 375 crosses German Creek in eastern Grainger County.

Below: A few covered bridges remain in Appalachia and illustrate a common practice of protecting the wood structures. This is the restored Doe River Covered Bridge in Elizabethton, Tennessee.

Covered bridges were once widely used in rural areas of Appalachia but have all but disappeared as steel-truss bridges and newer concrete bridges have replaced the older structures. Pictured is the Harrisburg Covered Bridge in Sevier County, Tennessee.

and could carry larger vehicles and heavier loads. The earlier steel-truss bridges were usually floored with wooden planks and would clatter as the vehicle would pass over. I can still hear the "clump-t-clump" of the boards as a car drove over the old structures. These venerable bridges had character and seemed to talk when crossed.

There are many types of bridge structures used throughout the world and in Appalachia. These include timber bridges, covered bridges, iron bridges, simple truss bridges, cantilever bridges, continuous truss bridges, continuous girder bridges, arch bridges, suspension bridges, concrete bridges, draw bridges and even pontoon bridges. Many of the early bridges in the Appalachian region were timber or wooden covered bridges.

Short-span concrete bridges and steel truss were the next most common types that could be seen in most areas but are now disappearing as more up-to-date design requirements are implemented into the construction of new bridges. One old concrete arch bridge still in use is in Knox County, where Mascot Road crosses the Holston River. This old bridge is picturesque and often seen on brochures and in photo contests. The concrete arches stand above the bridge deck in a smooth rolling pattern.

Bible Bridge, near the Greene County community of Warrensburg, exhibits the character of covered bridges, heavy wood beam construction covered with wood planks. The large structural wooden beams can be seen on the inside of the structure.

As these older bridges are replaced, most of the antiquated structures are dismantled and removed, mainly for safety and the cost of maintenance that would be required to keep the aging bridges functional. As time has passed by, most of the old bridges are now gone, with few exceptions.

At one time in East Tennessee and Appalachia, covered bridges were numerous and not mere beautiful structures to be admired. They served a purpose of providing protection of the wooden bridge structure, of course, from the elements. They were also extremely sturdy and strong, able to withstand much traffic and heavy weather. However, most wooden covered bridges have disappeared, some burned by vandals, others unmaintained and rotted.

It is not known how many wood-structured covered bridges once existed in the state, but only four are known to survive and continue to be used. Three of the four are in East Tennessee: the Elizabethton Bridge in Elizabethton, Harrisburg Bridge on Old State Highway 35 in Sevier County and Bible Bridge in Greene County. The other covered bridge is in Western Tennessee in Union City, Obion County.

The steel-truss highway bridges are rapidly disappearing and being replaced with new concrete and steel girder bridges. Some of the old

Covered bridges have all but disappeared in Appalachia. These windows provide illumination for drivers traveling through the covered bridge. Bible Bridge, near Warrensburg, Tennessee, Greene County.

steel-truss bridges can still be seen in Tennessee's Appalachian landscape. Beautifully constructed, they came in many designs, resembling tinker toy sets thrown up across broad East Tennessee rivers. One such bridge, about five hundred feet in length, is located on State Route 375 where it crosses German Creek near Bean Station in Grainger County. One of the more popular was the through-truss steel bridge at Reliance, Tennessee, removed and replaced with a flat cement bridge. Another steel-truss bridge is the Talley Bridge in Hancock County, where State Route 70 crosses the Clinch River. This bridge is scheduled to be replaced and may not be around much longer.

A country drive in Appalachia may take one across one of these old bridges, bringing back good memories of days gone by. Slowly, these old structures are disappearing as new improved highways are constructed. Hearing that clatter of boards or a groan of stress from the old bridges was always a thrill as a young child. All had their own personality and unusual-looking structure. The character of these old relics is what I miss the most: their blending with the countryside, the texture of the wood beams or rusted yellowish-red steel truss overhead, even the gray weathered wood. Yes, those days are fast disappearing.

21

RIVER FERRIES

Older rivers flow slowly, sometimes moving at what seems like glacial speed. Younger rivers tend to be fast flowing, tumbling and awash in "white water" as they course their way downward ever closer to sea level. As the landscape changes through time so do the rivers change with time, always trying to get to a lower level, sea level.

"Come on up the ramp, but drive slowly," the ferry captain said. We would creep to the end of the ferry with the car and put the vehicle's emergency brake on. "Okay y'all hold tight. We're going to take off now." We can hear the thump of the motor that propels this ferry across the river. It is an old diesel engine. Some ferries used mules to pull the ferry across a river, guided by a cable fastened to large trees or anchored into the ground. Other ferries used the river current to adroitly maneuver the ferry across the body of moving water. "Okay folks hold on. We are going to go ashore with a thump," the captain said. Slowly, the ferry boat swung around and gently glided into the man-made dock. We got in our car and slowly drove off the floating bridge and back onto dry land.

One of the old types of river crossings is all but gone today. Ferries were once a common way to cross rivers, but today they have disappeared from the highway landscape. Some people used them daily to go to work, as they may have lived on the other side of a river from their employment location. Farmers would often use ferries to transport equipment from a field on one side of the river to a field on the other side. Livestock was also transported across rivers, as farmers would move their livestock to different pastures or even to transport them to the market for sale.

Along the Holston River between Grainger County and Jefferson County, there were as many as twenty ferry crossings at one time in the late 1800s and into the 1900s. Many were named for the family that operated the ferry business. Others were named for the location of the ferry. Examples include the Nance Ferry, named after the Nance family who owned the land along the river. Another was Indian Cave Ferry, after the large cave feature on the Grainger County side of the Holston River. Both ferries are long gone today.

In the early days, the cost of taking a ferry might have been a half-dozen eggs, or a laying hen, or a bale of hay. The method of payment changed through time and ended up being currency, with costs as high as ten cents per trip in the 1920s and 1930s and going up to several dollars in later years in the 1950s and 1960s. Children usually enjoyed the trip across the river, as it was an adventure, not unlike the Huck Finn stories. Sometimes the trip across was fast due to heavy currents or a storm; other times the trip may have taken a wrong turn if the cable broke, causing the floating barge to run aground in the wrong location. Most of the time, people and vehicles were transported across rivers without incident.

I miss that old-time method of crossing the rivers in Appalachia. I rode across a few ferries as a child, but they quickly disappeared as the 1950s ended. This unique method of transportation has quietly vanished from our lives in Appalachia. Young people today will never know the unique and thrilling way cars used to cross rivers. Today, concrete and steel bridges now carry the load of transporting people and cars and trucks across rivers, safer and quicker. The disappearance of Appalachia is marked by the absence of the old river ferry.

22
WILSON NANCE AND NANCE'S FERRY

Wilson Nance, who is not much larger than a boat oar, sits in a gray cane back chair on his nephew's front porch. Curve-tailed black dogs and chickens scratch and scramble on the roadside for fun and food.

It is early morning on the river, and some light fog lingers in the trees, bushes and river on Nance's Ferry Road.

Wilson Nance, eighty-six years old at the time of this interview, is contemplative, as still as a stone, as he stares across the road to rich red bottomland planted in tobacco and watermelons. He looks on beyond to the river. The bottoms up from the mouth of Lost Creek and the river were part of his family for more than two hundred years.

Since the late 1700s, there has always been a Nance in this section of Jefferson County. And for much of that time, a Nance has either operated a ferry across the Holston River or rented the operation to someone who did.

The ferry has been important not only for moving people and equipment, but it has also served as a geographical and cultural bridge between Jefferson and Grainger Counties. At the time of this interview, the ferry is but a distant memory for Wilson Nance and those who rode it regularly. The ferry lies rotting and rusting underneath a tree on the banks of the Holston River, where it once tied up. Returning to the river appears to be a fading hope.

Wilson began working the farm and the river as a boy, but it was the river that shaped his fondest memories. Farm work was hard and long and not

Nance's Ferry, shown here, operated on the Holston River between Grainger and Jefferson Counties. The ferry operated for over five generations and ceased operation in the 1970s. *Courtesy of David Mitchell.*

nearly as much fun as moving people, animals and other things across the bristling river.

And it was always the two endeavors, farming and ferrying. Never just one or the other. Wilson Nance divided his time and energies between cows and crossings. River water was in his blood. His ancestors landed on the Holston and its rambling green hillsides in Jefferson County before America's independence. When the first Nance claimed the hills, nearby Indian tribes became more aggressive about the intrusion.

Sitting straight as a rod in the cane back chair, Wilson says he does not know too much about the first Nances who settled the area.

Tony Holmes, a senior technical services specialist with the Tennessee Valley Authority, wrote extensively on Tennessee's vanishing ferries. The Nance ferry was one that caught his eye. Holmes discovered the Nance family was originally from Nancy, France. They changed their name to Nance. Three Nancy brothers migrated from France in the early to mid-1770s, landing in Louisiana.

Two of the brothers traveled east, and one trekked west. One of the two brothers stopped in Grainger County, and the other crossed the river at the ferry point, pushing the Indians back.

This late 1960s photo shows the Mitchell family of Grainger County crossing the Holston River on Nance's Ferry. These old ferries are all but gone in Appalachia, replaced with new concrete and steel-beam bridges. *Courtesy of David Mitchell.*

The river crossing was on a trace used by early pioneers heading west. There is evidence Cherokee Indians used the crossing, but the Nance brothers set up the first commercial ferry at the crossing.

What was a dirt road in the beginning is paved today and runs in front of the only place Nance has lived. In many ways, the road and river have given him a rich view of life. Wilson Nance was named for his uncle Will Nance, who operated the ferry before renting it to Tody Willings. Wilson Nance says he was quite fond of his uncle, who owned the farm and then handed it down.

Wilson's father, Bert, ran the ferry before him. Bert's father, Jeff, operated it before his son. After that rundown on the ferry's history, you run out of Wilson's memory.

Published accounts record that in the times when the frontier was young and full of roaming Indians, men on either side of the river watched offshore. Raising a white flag meant it was safe to cross. A red flag signaled that hostile Indians were in the vicinity.

The first ferry, Holmes wrote, was a log raft with a split log gunwale latched with wooden pegs. Two men on long oars fought the current, hoping to hit the designated landing on the opposite shore, which was not always possible.

Nance remembers "waterpower" and hand-walking the fifty-four-foot ferry across the river. Its metal hull supported planking on top, and a ship's wooden wheel reeled in the cable and steered the ferry. The idea was to aim the boat's bow upriver when crossing from Jefferson County into Grainger County and downriver when returning.

"I was going to the free [public] school, walking two miles up the road and back. I would work the ferry in the morning before school and in the afternoon after school." Well, almost. He worked in the fields in the afternoon as well. When he heard someone hollering to be hauled across the water, Wilson Nance would set off running.

Sometimes he ran a mile or more from the plowed fields to scoot the ferry across the river. He recalls plowing on days so hot that the fields blistered his bare feet. The ferry was a welcome relief.

"I began planting that bottom out there when I was nine years old with two old black mules and a cultivator. People came along the hard way in this country." he said. "Will Nance owned 184 acres. This is Nance land and has never been sold," he added.

In his memory, the first Nance was a John Nance. Records indicate that John originally purchased some one hundred acres for "18 shillings" as a down payment. The land was identified as being in the "first bottom above the mouth of Lost Creek."

"There have been five generations of Nances operating the ferry," Wilson said.

The ferry was his passion, the first thing he thought about in the morning and the last thing he checked on at night. There are stories of his rising from bed as early as 2:00 a.m. when he heard someone honking a car horn, needing to be ferried across the river.

In the early days, the charge was twenty cents for a horse and buggy and ten cents for a rider on horseback. Later, the price changed to twenty-five cents. In the ferry's last days in the late 1970s, Wilson Nance collected only fifty cents for a crossing. He apologized often for charging that much on a trip that took two minutes. But to go from Blaine in Grainger County to, say, New Market, by land was more than a twenty-five-mile trip one way.

The completion of Cherokee Dam in 1941, about twenty-five miles upriver from the ferry landing, just about put the operation out of business. It was difficult to judge the rise and fall of the water.

When the river was up, the ferry used the water's current. When the water was at its lowest, the ferry moved on a strong overhead cable stretched between both shores.

At times, Wilson Nance pulled the cable across the 350-foot-wide crossing, where in places the river was 8 feet deep. "Oh, there were some close calls," he said. "The boat has sunk with cattle or with trucks. There was plenty bad weather. The river would freeze over. I have seen ice tides on this river." Wilson Nance explained that an ice tide is when the river is frozen solid from top to bottom.

The ferry is mere memory today.

Down in the flicking shadows of the elms, sycamores and hackberry trees, the water runs in a comfortable fashion near the old ferry crossing. Cows graze on the hills.

23
OLD CARS

A great moment in life comes when the family finally owns an automobile. That does sound quaint, but at one time, purchasing a car was a big deal, and not a mega horn–blasting deal by a car salesman. The old automobile was big, roomy, large and drank up the gas, which was purchased by the cent instead of the dollar, as today. Today, those same old cars are mostly found in abandoned lots, cannibalized for parts long ago. They rust and even have trees growing up through their innards. But, oh, the stories they could tell of a time when the car was king, displacing the wagon and mule or horse.

The first cars in East Tennessee were top-heavy boxy things, like a man's top hat. In the mid-twentieth century, the car took on fenders that resembled fish fins or something that should have been on a rocket ship. They were engineered to a particular design each year, instead of looking as if they have been turned out by a robotic cookie cutter.

Year after year the cars were becoming more distinctive as to the make and model. A common pastime was to try to identify cars as they passed by: "Oh, that is a 1940 Ford Deluxe, I can tell by the grill and taillights," or "That, my friend, is a 1955 Chevy Bel Air, sporting a 283-cubic-inch V-8 motor." The youth of the mid-twentieth century were enamored with cars, especially the sporty and fast types. Many would buy older cars and repair and "modify" them to go faster and be more appealing.

A casualty from this grand interest in cars was the landscape. As more and more cars were produced, people would discard the older cars for

This 1940 Ford sits rusting away with other vintage automobiles in an unmarked junkyard in East Tennessee. These old cars are all but gone except for the cars and trucks that have been salvaged by enthusiasts.

newer ones. As a result, large, widespread junkyards of automobile hulks sprang up around the countryside, cars stacked next to one another and some even on top of each other. These unsightly automobile graveyards quickly became eyesores. With public support, these junkyards have all but disappeared from the Appalachian landscape, most having their rusty hulks recycled into fresh metal for automobiles of today.

PART V

MILLS, BARNS, OLD HOUSES AND RAILROADS

24
MILLS

A hardy class of European people mainly from England, Scotland, Ireland, Wales and Germany left their homelands in a restless urge to fill the hooks and faults, short valleys and sweeping hillsides in the first surges of restive clans who were undaunted by the vast, raw wilderness of upper East Tennessee.

They traveled into the wilds, a righteous people on a righteous mission, carrying with them hopes and dreams of future generations. Settlers had to have several attributes to survive: courage, luck, guts and knowhow.

Not least of these was the ability to make bar iron in a forge. Iron was as necessary as food, maybe more. Without iron for musket barrels and knives, the hard realities of the wilderness would have been too much to overcome in the unforgiving backcountry. Here lurked danger in natural abundance and in Indian tribes who viewed the intrusion of Europeans as a dark and dangerous time in their existence.

In the first years of settlement and farming, some small iron forges and water-powered gristmills were the main venues of work.

FRENCH'S MILL

French's Mill, one of the earliest listed in Tennessee, is also known as Dumplin Bloomery Forge. The overshot waterwheel mill is located just off French Mill Road in Jefferson County. Dumplin Creek feeds the waterwheel today as it did in the late 1790s or early 1800s, when the mill was built.

At this writing, the mill is owned by Freeman Lambright, seventy-one at the time of the interview. Lambright is an Amish blacksmith who has restored the old mill, using all its original belts, pulleys, gears, wheels, beams and resources that were available in pioneer times in Jefferson County.

He says the mill was first constructed by a family named Perkins. The Perkins Iron Works created an iron furnace where iron ore was melted.

The land where the mill is located was purchased around 1796, Lambright says. The mill also had an up-and-down sash saw to saw timbers. Along about 1825, the mill went out of business and was sold at auction. Later, it became a gristmill instead of an iron forge, employing millstones for grinding meal. At one stage of its existence, the old building and waterwheel served as a roller mill. That operation ceased about 1979, according to Lambright.

Lambright has replaced the grinding stones and grinds meal today as it was once done so long ago. There is no charge for the small bags of meal, but donations to help with the mill are welcome.

The mill itself is large, standing about three stories tall. It is painted bright red, but inside the structure Lambright has used all his skills as a blacksmith and a former Sears service technician to restore the mill using as much of the original equipment as possible.

Lambright purchased the mill in 1990 and began his restoration of the building, the gearing, all the belts and pulleys. He acquired two grinding stones and made them into vertical grinders and has been grinding meal for about four years.

"I'm still practicing and learning," he said.

Although there is no charge for entering the mill to see how it operates, he does accept donations. "All the stuff is original, except one of the grinders. I bought it at an antique place. It was out in the rain and weather and I rescued it. That is the only new piece of equipment that is not original."

He transformed the operation from a gear drive to a belt drive. He says the big gear on the eighteen-foot waterwheel drove a spur gear. "I ran a shaft and pully on the shaft to drive it that way." Previously, the gears were subject to dirt from the water running over the overshot buckets.

The early operation, Lambright says, used a five-hundred-pound trip hammer to hammer iron into bars. It was a crude operation, like many found in southeastern Tennessee and North Carolina.

"Coal had not been found, so they had to use charcoal to keep it hot enough [to melt the ore]. They pumped air with a bellows with waterpower.

"They had dug a hole, called a put furnace. They put in over two feet of charcoal and three feet of iron ore and covered that with clay to make a

Above: French's Mill in Jefferson County is one of a handful of working gristmills left in the East Tennessee area. Its owner has rebuilt several structural elements of the mill, including the millwheel and pulley system.

Right: The current owner (as of this writing) of French's Mill in Jefferson County, Freeman Lambright, discusses the numerous repairs he has made on the old structure.

The main wheel and belts are shown in action at French's Mill. The interior wheel is powered by the turning water wheel outside of the mill and connected directly to this wheel.

This is the main wheel that drives all the other pulleys and belts in the mill. It is connected to the main water wheel on the outside of the structure.

Ground grain is placed in these paper bags at French's Mill in Jefferson County. In times past, ground meal often was poured into cloth sacks for delivery.

dome. They would light the charcoal and blow air until they got a big glob of iron and carbon mixed. They put that inside a chafery forge [to reheat the iron]. Then they hammered all the carbon out of it and sold that to blacksmiths."

The wrought iron was then turned into knives and barrels for muskets, necessary tools on the frontier.

Lambright grew up working in a blacksmith shop in LaGrange County, Indiana, where about 70 percent of the population is Amish and still speak Pennsylvania Dutch, a mixture of German, Holland Dutch, Swiss and English. Lambright speaks it fluently.

COX MILL

Located in the Mill Springs community of Jefferson County is one of the oldest standing mills in the East Tennessee region. Although the exterior and structural framework has been recently restored, it still has the look from when it was last used in the 1950s.

The mill was thought to have been built in 1803 and was advertised that way for many years. It was known as Cox Mill, named after the owner, William Cox, who bought land in Mill Springs in 1796. It later became known as Mill Springs Mill and retains that name today. William Cox owned approximately 2,500 acres in and around the Mill Springs community.

According to Jefferson County records, Cox was appointed Jefferson County magistrate by Governor William Blount in 1792 and again by Governor John Sevier in 1796. Cox also voted for the formation of the Lost State of Franklin, whose governor was John Sevier in 1784. The State of Franklin was an unsuccessful effort by Greene and Washington Counties in upper East Tennessee, headed by John Sevier and others, to form a new state between Virginia and North Carolina.

There is some question about whether William Cox built the mill. Cox's will was probated in 1805, and the mill was listed as part of his estate, but there is no mention of who actually built the gristmill. Recent research by the National Historic Trust dates the mill's construction in 1792, based on pencil marks found on the brick mortar joints by a masonry expert and researcher. Those marks, white pencil lines, were poplar during the early 1790s masonry construction. Records and community history indicate that the Mill Springs Mill ran continuously, twenty-four hours a day, except for maintenance and repairs. It was operated for over 153 years into the 1950s.

Above: Cox Mill was last operated in the 1950s and is shown here from the late 1940s. It was an under-shot mill, where the water from the millrace fed into the lower slots of the water wheel, turning the wheel back toward the incoming water. *Courtesy of Linda Gass.*

Opposite, top: Today the old mill in Mill Springs (Cox Mill) still stands, but the water wheel is not connected and does not operate.

Opposite, bottom: The all-brick gristmill is only one of two entirely brick mills in Tennessee. This photo shows a commonly used tie bolt to aid in keeping the brick wall stable.

The most unusual part of the mill's history is in its architecture. Most of the mills of that period were built of logs or wood-frame construction or stone, whereas Cox's Mill is entirely brick. According to Cox family tradition, it was said to have been built with bricks made by slaves. It was also an under-shot mill, where the water from the millrace fed into the lower slots of the water wheel, turning the wheel back toward the incoming water. The mill is only one of two brick mills to have survived in the state of Tennessee from the early 1800s. The two-story brick mill was operated by Dick Howard for several years during the late 1940s and 1950s, according to Libby Neely and Jim Talley, who lived in the community.

The mill stands at the junction of River Road and Fielden Store Road (also referred to as Mill Springs Road during the 1940s and 1950s). The road was a narrow and curvy gravel road up until the late 1950s, when it was tarred and chipped with small gravel to make a paved road, still narrow and curvy. Before the road was later paved, it was oiled every year to keep the dust down to tolerable levels.

25
BARNS

The barn in East Tennessee captures a romantic time in the history of the Appalachian region. The author was once told by a farmer that his father told him to build the barn first and the barn would build his house. Barns in this region come in so many varieties and sizes, from small structures that housed a family's meat (smokehouse) to massive buildings for multiple uses. Many have withstood the elements and can be seen today on lonely patrol in a field, on the side of a road or wide-spanning highway. Aging gray barns

Farm implements are commonly hung on the side or front of outbuildings and barns in the rural Appalachian area such as shown here on a barn in Carter County, Tennessee.

Barns take many shapes and designs in the rural area of Appalachia. Many barns have "faces" as one looks at them from afar, such as this one in Hamblen County.

Many barns in Appalachia are used for both livestock and hay storage such as this one in east Knox County along highway 11-W.

Cantilevered barns were once common in the Appalachian area as shown here in the Richardson Cove section of Sevier County. Look closely in the shadows, and you'll see that this barn is a log structure.

Many old barns are constructed of plank-style wood siding with vents in the apex of the roofline for ventilation. This Anderson County barn uses four diamond-shaped holes cut into the wood siding.

This photo clearly shows the cantilever nature of the barn structure. The overhanging level provides extra shelter for storing materials and farm equipment while livestock are quartered in the enclosed substructure.

Neglect and abandonment cause once beautiful and useable barns to decay and collapse into themselves.

This scene is fast being lost to time as more and more people move into the cities and leave the rural life. This four-cornered log crib-style barn is a rare structure to be seen in this area, Anderson County.

Many old barns are of simple construction and have only a central opening for access to the interior, like this barn in Greene County, Tennessee.

Silos were once a common sight on farms in the Appalachian area. They are fast disappearing from the landscape. These silos, located on a previous dairy farm in Jefferson County, are slowly being overtaken by vines and other vegetation as family-owned dairy farms are mostly gone from the Appalachian landscape.

This cantilever barn, located in Unicoi County, is still being used today and is very well preserved.

Many old barns in Appalachia have advertisements painted on their roofs. Most are now gone; a few still advertise "See Rock City," but they are fast disappearing.

Old dilapidated wood structures usually conceal treasures of our past, such as this old farm cultivator that was a horse-drawn implement, found in a lean-to structure on a barn in rural Anderson County.

speak of another time. Some were even designed to obviate local taxes. They are known as cantilever barns, in which only the part of the structure that was on the ground was taxed. Tobacco barns were prevalent in East Tennessee but have faded with the time. Barns provided shelter for work animals and hay, not to mention chickens and stray cats and the occasional rusty antique automobile.

26
HOUSES

It is hard to miss the wraparound porches of early farm homes in East Tennessee. The log cabin was here long before homes took on the look of modernity with wood siding. But farmhouses, some of which were covered log cabin buildings, have a definite simple but efficient appearance, unlike today's mega homes. Houses were utilitarian in design, just like the farmers themselves, who most often built their own homes on land purchased for one purpose—farming.

Appalachian homesteads were typically log structures and framed board-and-batten cabins. Outbuildings were also a part of the farmstead and included smokehouses (*above right*) for curing pork.

This is an example of a rural farmhouse from the mid-twentieth century in rural Appalachia. These old homes are usually left to disrepair and eventual demolition.

An old log cabin and frame attachment still stand on the hillside along Hogskin Road in Grainger County. The stories that could be told by this cabin are limitless and would extend back well over one hundred years.

Log cabins are all but gone in the landscape except for newly restored and new construction cabins, mainly in the tourist areas. This cabin rests out its remaining days in the brush of Sevier County.

Settlers initially built log homes in the Appalachian region, and some still remain intact, as this old log structure illustrates. This old home was last lived in around the late 1930s and is found alongside U.S. Highway 11-W south of Rutledge, Tennessee.

As the Appalachian culture disappears so does evidence of the culture such as old farm home places, most of which are falling into disrepair.

Past homes from the rural Appalachian landscape were often of framed construction, simple and small considering today's standards. Board-and-batten siding was in common use in the early 1900s but is rarely used today.

Most farmhouses in Appalachia had a back porch where clothes washing and some food preparation would take place, like this house in rural Cocke County.

A screened-in back porch was a coveted place during the hot summer months when flying insects would make one's life miserable outside.

Above: Many early houses in Appalachia were of log construction, such as this log house in the Porters Creek section of the Smoky Mountains National Park.

Left: A common fixture on any rural homestead in the Appalachian region during days gone by was the outhouse. This was the bathroom for the home in the early days and usually consisted of a small wooden building with a one- or two-seated commode and a supply of catalogues and a fly swatter. Indoor plumbing quickly did away with these once prominent fixtures.

27

RAILROADS FORGOTTEN

I remember when I was a young boy growing up in the rural part of South Knoxville, I would occasionally walk along the small railroad tracks that reached into the marble and rock quarry district of Island Home. Walking the rail tracks was a hard affair, as the crossties were not spaced evenly for a person to step on. I might get two or three in a row, but eventually I would have to take a giant step or a mini step to get back on the ties. Most of the ties were old, gray and weather-beaten, as this line was not a heavily traveled route.

Several of my friends always speculated on why the spacing of the railroad ties were the way they were. Maybe the people who built the railroad tracks had shorter legs than we did so they could walk on them with ease, we incorrectly assumed. Whatever the reason, the railroad tracks had a special purpose, and everyone knew where they were located and usually when a train was going to be traveling by.

I saw my first real big passenger train in downtown Knoxville when I was five or six years old. We had to take the train to West Virginia one time, and we boarded the train at the old L&N Train Station along the Second Creek valley in Knoxville. The roar and rumble of the big train engines fascinated me as a child. The earth would shake as the train moved, and the sound was deafening at times. The trains were the main mass transit system, next to bus lines, for people traveling to other big cities and other states.

I vaguely remember the steam locomotive as a child but saw only a few in operation. Most of the railroad locomotives had changed to diesel for fuel by the 1950s and 1960s.

In the early twentieth century, Appalachia was accessed mainly by riverboats, horseback, dirt roads and railroads. At one time, many railroad lines were established in East Tennessee as the rich mineral and timber resources were mined and harvested and transported out of the region to large industrial areas in the Northeast. Most all these early railroad lines have now disappeared, only an occasional abandoned railroad bed can be seen.

A few of the rail lines that were busy transporting people and products around East Tennessee included the old Smoky Mountain Railroad, which ran from Vestal in South Knoxville to Sevierville. The rail line ran through Shooks Gap at the Knox and Sevier County line. Also traversing Shooks Gap was the main road to Sevierville and the Smoky Mountains, Chapman Highway (US 441).

Some of the other railroad lines in the East Tennessee area as described by Elmer Sulzer, author of *Ghost Railroads of Tennessee*, include the Peavine Railroad (later the Southern Railroad), Little River Railroad, East Tennessee and Western North Carolina Railroad, Beaver Dam Railroad, Fountain Head Railroad, Emory River Railroad, Pigeon River Railroad, Holston Valley Railroad and the famous Southern Railroad and Louisville and Nashville Railroad (L&N). Very few remnants of these old rail lines are left today, with an occasional distinctive railroad bed seen in the rural landscape.

One of the more memorable railroads to me was the old Smoky Mountain Railroad. It was the rail line that carried people and freight between Vestal and Sevierville. It crossed the Knox and Sevier County line at Shooks Gap in Seymour, Tennessee. As I was raised in the Island Home section of South Knoxville, we would travel out Chapman Highway to visit friends in Seymour and travel to the Smoky Mountains. When the Smoky Mountain Railroad line was still in use in the late 1950s, the conductor would have to light a flare and stop traffic on Chapman Highway at Shooks Gap so the train could traverse the gap. On January 16, 1961, all operations on the Smoky Mountain Railroad were embargoed, and in December 1963, application was made to abandon the rail line, which became effective in May 1964.

What I remember most about the old Smoky Mountain Railroad was that after the railroad shut down, an old locomotive, No. 110, was left on the tracks at Shooks Gap, where it was later vandalized and left to rust away. I traveled out Chapman Highway many times in my youth and saw that old locomotive engine sitting there, resolute to withstand time and weather. I eventually photographed it one day in 1970 because I felt that it was a part of our heritage that would soon disappear.

Locomotive engine No. 110 of the Smoky Mountain Railroad sits abandoned on old tracks at Shooks Gap at the Knox and Sevier County line, 1970. The rail line was closed in 1964, and No. 110 was left to the elements.

Shown here is a seldom seen photo of a steam locomotive from the TVA construction site of Cherokee Dam in Jefferson County, late 1930s. *Courtesy of the Tennessee State Library and Archives and the Tennessee Valley Authority archives.*

In May 1972, a young college engineering student named Terry Bloom acquired the old locomotive for around $3,000. It was taken to Brookville, Ohio, where Bloom was from, for restoration.

Many of the old railroads in Appalachia were used to haul lumber or coal out of the region. The rail lines were famous in the first half of the twentieth century but have since faded to only distant memories. The disappearing of Appalachia has left shadows of its past along the way, including the old railroad lines that once crossed East Tennessee's landscape.

PART VI

APPALACHIAN MUSIC

28

A UNIQUE SOUND

I love the sound of the plucking banjo, the high-pitched strumming of the mandolin, the beat of an upright bass and the picking of that standard of music, the guitar. Hearing the rhythm of the bluegrass band is like listening to the roll of a wave in the ocean. It makes the soul move deep inside one's chest. It distinguishes the culture of the mountain land from the rest of the country.

Banjo music is Appalachian music and can be found in most all bluegrass music groups.

Although Appalachian music has not disappeared, many of the old musical instruments have. Guitars, banjos, mandolins, fiddles, upright bases and dobros (shown) constitute the traditional bluegrass/Appalachian music instrument ensemble. Most of the original instruments have disappeared, replaced with more modern-made pieces.

Appalachian music combines the ballads and storytelling into a cacophony of tunes and sounds that has enriched the culture of the land we call Appalachia. Bluegrass, mountain music, spirituals and gospels are combined into a sound that is unique to the ridges and valleys of the Appalachian region.

PART VII

EPILOGUE

29

FINAL THOUGHTS

The soft breeze bends the yellow flower stems in a uniform fashion. The mountain-like ridge across the way shadows the lower valley as the low sun begins its decent in the west. Barn roofs counter play with farmhouses and other outbuildings, providing a texture to the rolling landscape. Small animals scurry along the forest floor locating their den for the night. A brilliant orange-red palate reflects off the late evening clouds as I descend off the flank of Clinch Mountain.

Appalachia spreads across many ridges, valleys, plateaus and mountains in this region of the United States. These mountains have beckoned humans to explore their environs for millennia, long before "white man" ever walked this terrain. The natural resources and wilderness drew European explorers and settlers to this area in competition with the established Native Americans and their culture.

Through the millions of years before humans, Appalachia began to change, slowly over time, and at an imperceptible pace. As we know today, change is constant. Forces in our universe consistently and constantly transform our surroundings, the natural order of life, into something else—maybe new, maybe a slightly different version of the former, things that once were, are now different and disappearing.

The Appalachian Mountains, thought once to be thousands of feet high, have slowly eroded to the residual mountains we see today. Their majesty lies in their gentleness and life-sustaining qualities that have supported humans for many thousands of years: trees for housing, stone for building, wildlife for food and fresh water for drinking.

As the mountains weather downward, so does the vegetation change, and wildlife evolves into new forms adapting to the changing environment. Slowly, over time, the Appalachian Mountains have changed, transforming into something different than before, or simply disappearing.

Change is not limited to the natural world. Humans have lived in these mountains for thousands of years. More recently, European settlers entered the Appalachian region several hundred years ago, establishing villages, towns and cities. They introduced their European way of life into the mountains and valleys of East Tennessee's Appalachia, birthing an Appalachian culture.

To view the Appalachian culture of the ninetieth and twentieth centuries, one must give attention to that way of life, how they thought, what they valued and cherished. They expressed these virtues in their music, religion, art and even language. Some of these intangibles were expressed in their artifacts: the churches, old dwellings, shops and implements that were left behind as their culture disappeared.

Our purpose with this effort was to capture a slice of history in the flow of time of Appalachian life in East Tennessee, a time of exploration and discovery; inventing tools, music and architecture; spiritual wellbeing; and education. By interviewing people who lived in the early twentieth century, we feel that we have captured a portion of what it was like back in the day. Their connection with the land and their forefathers has distilled in our narrative the spirit of Appalachian life in those times—a way of life that has all but disappeared. Their experience of change brings us awareness of what we have today, materially and spiritually.

A recurring theme from our interviews was that the most eventful, beneficial change to Appalachia was the introduction of electricity. Almost all those we talked with repeatedly said "getting electricity" was the best thing that has happened to this region in their lifetime. It was said that instead of using an oil lamp or light from a fireplace fire, the family could stay up, sit around a table and talk.

Others said that families would sit around a radio and listen to the news or to music. A favorite nightly pastime was reading from the family Bible by electric light. One person commented that they could see who was at home at night by the light coming from the windows of the distant farmhouses.

A close second to electricity was the indoor toilet. It was said that there was nothing like having to go to the outhouse during the night in ten-degree cold to use a slick page from a Sears and Roebuck catalogue. "Yes indeed! Indoor toilets were a Godsend!"

To that end, the advent of the Tennessee Valley Authority not only reduced flooding in the East Tennessee region but also brought electricity and a better life for the people, especially rural populations. As time moved forward, more and more homes began to use electric appliances like washing machines, electric stoves (ranges), whole house lighting and eventually electric heat and air condition.

Another obvious change in the Appalachian landscape was the disappearance of the country store. These general merchandise stores served the local communities. They provided easy access to foodstuffs, hardware items and gasoline/diesel fuel. Some served as the post office and a local gathering place. Large chain and box stores effectively ended the country store's existence as the twentieth century began to evolve into a more urban society.

As the population grew, the rural communities of Appalachia disappeared into towns and cities. Urban life changed into suburban life and then came suburban sprawl, in which rows of cookie-cutter homes and McMansions spread across the landscape. Community schools were consolidated into large county school systems, taking the education out of the small, rural community. As one ninety-year-old interviewee said, "When they took the schools out of their communities, that's when our country began to go down!"

Technology changed agriculture. What used to be done in a day or two with a set of mules and a man or two can now be accomplished with today's technology in an hour or less. Fifty acres was a good-sized farm a century ago. Today, a farmer can cultivate two thousand acres almost by himself. Corporate farms today often comprise ten thousand acres or more, as the small family farm has disappeared from Appalachia. More food can be produced today by fewer farmers due to technology. Multi-row machines can farm an acre of ground in less time than it takes a person to read the front page of a newspaper. Today, U.S. farmers feed not only America but also other parts of the world.

We also found that not everything new is bad. Our road system is one of the best in the world. Solid paved roads and superhighways allow the population to move about unencumbered. Farmers can transport products to markets and to the populace much quicker with less expense. Safe and sound engineering has provided key river crossings for roads and railways. In Appalachia, paved highways were especially important in economic growth, replacing curvy dirt and gravel roads.

Modernization of the previously mentioned electric system, communication networks and medical and dental facilities is by far a profound advancement for the people of Appalachia. Good health brings the population to a better life. As time moved ahead, the quality of living conditions also improved, allowing families to prosper.

At one time, agriculture and manufacturing were the heart of Appalachian economic growth. Today, most of those jobs have disappeared. Change occurs rapidly in our lives today, and the hope is that it is a positive change going forward. Some of the more negative attributes of today's culture indicated to the authors were the use of drugs and alcohol and the onset of television.

From the changes in our geological landscape to the fluctuations in Appalachian culture, our place in the Appalachian region has changed. Some believe for the better, others say for the worse. The past is vanishing, and the new will soon not know the best of those past times. The music from the heart, the spiritual goodness from the soul, the folk tales, stories and history all characterize aspects of the Appalachian life, a life that is changing, a life that is disappearing.

Deep in the southern Appalachians, we are always looking back. It is a longing for things that have vanished: country stores, dirt roads, gear-shift trucks, down around the bend, creeks full of fish, ringer washers, big trees, grasshoppers in tall weeds.

That never ends. We tend to believe that we have missed something important. Maybe we even hear the clatter from way back, people laughing, crying, life happening.

We are haunted by the past in the South. Author, novelist and icon William Faulkner was said to wistfully look over his shoulder, realizing he had missed something big. The Civil War was that something big. He regretted having been born too late to see the war for himself, to write of it firsthand.

It is that firsthand experience we need in the South. It is in our food that grandmothers cooked with loads of lard. It is in the way we walk or the way we look at our home place. It is a reverence that rarely occurs in other people. In the Southland, we feel the land's embrace.

We know each other in the South, and when something goes missing in our lives, we instantly understand it is gone.

Food is not only different in the South, but it is also better than any place on earth. We get the soil in our food here. No fluff. No air. It is real.

Love, too, is real in the South. When we say "Bless your heart," we really do mean bless your heart.

When we say, "come back to see us," we mean come back as soon as you can.

When we invite you into our home to eat with us, we mean come in and pull up a chair at our table.

We treat you so many ways in the South you are bound to like one of them.

So, when things go missing, when we look back, we ask, "Whatever happened to that old house down there around the bend, the one with all the big trees and open fields?" It hurts to learn that it has disappeared, faded into a row of houses that all look alike.

The family farms, in which every soul played a role, have vanished, along with stick-shift trucks and well water hauled in by buckets on a rope. A communal dipper was at the lip of the well, most of the time covered by a piece of wood planking.

Gone are old dogs that roll out from beneath the house and stretch before greeting strangers, sniffing the wind for friends.

Gone are red dirt roads, rumpled with ruts.

One of the most haunting sounds in the evening dusk was a mother calling in her children for supper. And it was supper, not dinner we ate around a table filled with parents, grandparents and any friends who might be passing by.

Nostalgia is a yearning for the past. But longing in the South is only partially related to nostalgia. We not only yearn for past surroundings but also understand that it will never be again. That knowledge tears at us as it does in no other place.

When we see an iron through-truss bridge still in use, we know that the past is alive, if only for a while longer. Wood bridges bring smiles, as do old water mills, where once corn was ground into meal for entire communities.

This is not nostalgia per se. It is a feeling for the way we were and wish we still had some of that past with us because now we know it was worth the effort to keep.

We no longer see wraparound porches on farm homes. Our friends and relatives rarely sit on a front porch and rock in large ladder-back rockers that creak in different rhythms.

There was nothing easy about working from daylight to dusk, milking cows, plowing long rows of cotton or corn or wheat or fescue or creating a large garden to be worked not with mule and plow but with a hoe and strong back.

It wasn't the farm work. It was bigger than that. It was the land. We were the land, and the land was us. We were the trees in the forest, and the trees fed us. We were the white, puffy skies, dotted with flocks of birds that have also disappeared.

There is a great sense of loss in the New South, where the past has been all but obliterated by modern shopping malls on the edges of towns.

But in this land where our ancestors are buried, where our lives are caught up in the land, where we look back and wonder what is all that sound back there, we will never forget.

What has disappeared is not gone from our hearts and minds. It is as fresh as the day we first recognized this place we call home was different and blessed.

30
SUNDRIES IN BLACK AND WHITE

Canning jars are a common sight in Appalachia. These jars stand in repose in a smokehouse ready for filling with tomatoes, cucumbers and beans.

Left: Outhouses were a common structure at most all homesteads in the Appalachian region, especially in the rural areas. These "outside bathrooms" are all but gone from the Appalachian landscape, replaced by the more adequate and sanitary plumbing in use today.

Below: Tractors are a mainstay of farming, replacing the oxen-, horse- and mule-driven equipment. Appearing on many rural farms in the late 1930s and 1940s, tractors greatly improved the ability of farmers to produce crops. Today, many of the old tractors are gone, replaced by new tractors, some that are computer-driven. Some of the older tractors can be seen rusting in the old fields and byways of Appalachia.

The rural Appalachian landscape is commonly marked by silos, often abandoned or unused. These prominent structures are often made of concrete, concrete blocks or bricks. This silo is found on the David Mitchell Farm in southwestern Grainger County.

Making apple butter was a common event in rural Appalachia. These cooking events usually occurred in the fall of the year in most communities. A few families and groups continue to make apple butter. Illustrated here is the process of adding sugar to the cooked apples and stirring with the wooden paddle.

An occasional barn or remote pasture field in rural East Tennessee may still hold a treasure for old-car enthusiasts.

A farm implement once found on most farms but now lost to our past is the manure spreader. This horse/mule-drawn machine would be used to spread livestock waste on cropland to provide fertilizer for the crops. Bullen Valley, Grainger County.

Burley tobacco used to be a common and widespread cash crop in the rural areas of Appalachia. This photo, made in Jefferson County, illustrates how the tobacco is hung in barns to cure before going to market.

Right: Smokehouses were once a staple of rural home places in Appalachia. Today, they have mostly disappeared, with those remaining being used for storage.

Below: Outbuildings and sheds were once common around homes and farmsteads. Most of these structures housed farm equipment, automobiles or trucks or doubled as a curing shed for fruits and vegetables. Most have fallen into disrepair and are becoming a rare fixture on the farm, Sevier County.

An old Ford hubcap and an iron bed headboard decorate the front of a smokehouse, Greene County.

This porch is supported with field stones collected in the adjacent pasture.

Outdoor drive-in theaters were once a popular attraction for many in the southern Appalachians. Today, these movie theaters have just about disappeared from the landscape. Pictured here is State Line Theater in Elizabethton, Tennessee.

Oil lamps were commonly used light sources in homes in Appalachia before the introduction of electricity. The variety of oil lamps was endless.

Above: Cast iron pots and pans were once the main cooking utensils when wood-burning stoves were used in the kitchen.

Right: Today cellphones are the main telephone type most use for communication. In Appalachia and elsewhere, the old crank wall phone was a common fixture in the home and in the local grocery; shown is Blaine IGA grocery, Grainger County, Tennessee.

Bed springs and a footboard rust in the remains of an old house in Appalachia, long since abandoned.

Remnants of a home are left in the woods where the house was once lived in. This old house was built of stone picked up around the surrounding area; the fireplace is in the center of the wall between the windows.

Smoking tobacco used to be sold in cans that were easily placed in a back pocket of someone's overalls or pants. Brand names in the early twentieth century have now disappeared.

At one time in the past, junkyards dotted the rural landscape. Today, they have been mostly demolished as the old junk cars have been sold as scrap metal. This car yard near Grimsley in Fentress County is meticulously kept and contains vintage cars from the 1940s to the 1950s.

These chimneys mark the site of an Appalachian farm home where these fireplaces provided the needed warmth for cold winter nights.

What was once a common fixture in the country kitchen, an egg basket, is now only found in antique stores and private collections. These baskets were hand woven, usually from white oak strips.

The lands of Appalachia whisper as the culture of the rural heritage slowly disappears from the landscape.

BIBLIOGRAPHY

Byerly, D.W. *The Last Billion Years, A Geologic History of Tennessee*. Knoxville: University of Tennessee Press, 2013.

Hatcher, R.D., Jr. "Tectonics of the Southern and Central Appalachian Internides." *Annual Review of Earth and Planetary Science* 15 (1987): 337–62.

Hatcher, R.D., Jr., C.E. Merschant, R.C. Milici and L.S. Wiener. "A Structural Transect in the Southern Appalachians, Tennessee and North Carolina." In *Field Trips in the Southern Appalachians: Tennessee Division of Geology Report of Investigations* No. 37, edited by R.C. Milici, 6–51. Tennessee Division of Geology, 1978.

Knoxville Journal. "Jefferson Caveman." March 25, 1956.

Marion, Steve. "Cox Mill Gets Historic Marker." *Standard Banner* (Jefferson City, TN), December 11, 2014.

Miller, R.A. *The Geologic History of Tennessee*. Bull. 74, Tennessee Division of Geology, 1974.

Montgomery, M.B., and J.S. Hall. *Dictionary of Smoky Mountain English*. Knoxville: University of Tennessee Press, 2004.

Moore, H.L. *The Bone Hunters, The Discovery of Miocene Fossils in Gray*. Knoxville: University of Tennessee Press, 2004.

———. *A Geologic Trip Across Tennessee by Interstate 40*. Knoxville: University of Tennessee Press, 1994.

———. *A Roadside Guide to the Geology of the Great Smoky Mountains National Park*. Knoxville: University of Tennessee Press, 1988.

Moore, H.L., and Fred Brown. *Discovering October Roads*. Knoxville: University of Tennessee Press, 2001.

Moulton, D.W. *Report of the State Highway Commissioner of Tennessee for the Biennium Ending June 30, 1960*. Nashville: Tennessee Department of Highways, 1960.

Muncy, Estle P. *People and Places of Jefferson County*. Rogersville: East Tennessee Printing Company, 1994.

Neely, Elizabeth "Libby." Personal communication about living in Mill Springs, Tennessee, and her memories of Ben Ballinger, 2013.

Pack, D.M. *Report of the State Highway Commissioner of Tennessee for the Biennium Ending June 30, 1964*. Nashville: Tennessee Department of Highways, 1964.

Sulzer, E.G. *Ghost Railroads of Tennessee*. Bloomington: Indiana University Press, 1975.

Talley, Jim. Personal communication about living in Mill Springs, Tennessee, and his memories of Ben Ballinger, 2013.

Tennessee State Highway Department (TSHD). *History of the Tennessee Highway Department*. Nashville: State of Tennessee, 1959.

ABOUT THE AUTHORS

FRED BROWN, retired senior writer for the *Knoxville News Sentinel*, was a working journalist for more than forty-five years. In that time, he reported on a wide variety of assignments that took him to endzones as a sportswriter, to editing a small-town daily in Arkansas, to war zones as an embedded reporter on general assignment and finally as a senior writer writing regional history and features. He continues to freelance.

Brown is a member of the Scripps Howard Hall of Fame, recipient of the Tennessee Associated Press Managing Editors Malcolm Law Trophy for Feature Writing, received a National Endowment for the Humanities Fellowship in Journalism at the University of Michigan (1983–84) and was named to the East Tennessee Writers Hall of Fame for excellence in journalism in 2008.

Besides his columns and stories for the *News Sentinel*, his publications include *The Serpent Handlers: Three Families and Their Faith* (John F. Blair Publishers, May 2000) and *Growing Up Southern* (Apocryphile Press), both coauthored with his late wife, Jeanne McDonald.

Among other nonfiction books authored by Brown are *Discovering October Roads*, with Harry Moore, and *Marking Time: The Stories behind East Tennessee's Historical Markers* (University of Tennessee Press).

Brown, a 1963 graduate of Presbyterian College, is currently working on a book that recounts two coalmine disasters of the early twentieth century in Coal Creek, Tennessee. He is also working on a book with Harry Moore about the disappearance of a way of life in East Tennessee's Appalachian culture.

Harry Moore, a graduate of the University of Tennessee, is a retired geologist from the Tennessee Department of Transportation (Knoxville) and more recently Golder Associates (Atlanta, Georgia), where he worked a combined forty-seven years studying the geology of East Tennessee and surrounding regions. He, as an engineering geologist, has been involved in the planning, design, construction and maintenance of East Tennessee's road system since 1972. His experience with landslides, rock falls, caves and sinkhole-related highway issues are known nationwide. He has penned numerous technical papers and made abundant presentations on not only highway engineering geology but the region's geology as well. He received the national Highway Geology Symposium Medallion Award for his contributions to the practice of highway engineering geology.

Harry, who grew up and lived in Knox and Grainger Counties, has authored several books, including *A Roadside Guide to the Geology of the Great Smoky Mountains National Park*, *A Geologic Trip across Tennessee by Interstate 40*, *Discovering October Roads* (coauthored with Fred Brown) and *The Bone Hunters* (all from University of Tennessee Press). He and his wife, Alice Ann, wrote a book about how World War II affected a small rural farming community in West Tennessee titled *The Lonely Road*.

Moore's knowledge of the Great Smoky Mountains National Park and East Tennessee culture and natural history is known regionally, where he has made numerous presentations to local groups about the region's geology.